1990

GEN 36...
McCorry, ...
Preventing substance abuse :

W9-ABS-843

3 0301 00069126 7

Preventing Substance Abuse:

A Comprehensive Program For Catholic Educators

Frank McCorry, Ph.D.

©1990, National Catholic Educational Association
Department of Elementary Schools
Washington, DC

ISBN 1 - 55833 - 040 - 5

LIBRARY
College of St. Francis
JOLIET, ILL.

LIBRARY
College of St. Francis
JOLIET, ILL.

362.29
M171

TABLE OF CONTENTS

6-11-90 Prelude #6.50

138, 193

DEDICATION

To Eddie Curry, my friend and relative, for his encouragement and affection. I shall remember you always.

ACKNOWLEDGEMENT

This book has many authors if only one writer. I wish to express my gratitude to some who come quickly to mind.

The students and families of the Catholic schools of the Archdiocese of New York who so openly shared themselves with me deserve special mention. They interested me in the realities of chemical dependency and in the need for effective prevention programs.

I also want to express my gratitude to the Archdiocese of New York Drug Abuse Prevention Program (ADAPP) especially Bob Charles and Sally Shields, the Directors of ADAPP, who preceded me and succeeded me in this position. They always exhibited a commitment to excellence and were fired with a passionate concern for youngsters. I would be remiss if I failed to mention two wonderful gentlemen who taught me the political intricacies of programming for a large independent school system, the late Monsignor James Feeney, and Brother James Kearney who served as Superintendent of Schools for the Archdiocese of New York.

I want to extend a special word of thanks to my wife, Margaret, and my daughters, Christine, Elizabeth, and Katie for their patience and unwavering support during this project. A special acknowledgement is in order for my son, Timothy, who had the good sense to delay his arrival until the initial draft of this work was completed. He has warmed our spirits since his coming.

I want to thank Robert Kealey, Ed.D., who drafted me for this assignment and who was a source of encouragement and assistance throughout.

Frank McCorry
January 1, 1990

PREFACE

The offices of the National Catholic Educational Association (NCEA) are located in Washington, DC. The national press has labeled the capital of the United States the "murder capital." Each year the number of killings continues to rise. The Washington police department has indicated that over 80% of the homicides are drug related. This percent is probably true of most large and small cities across the United States. Is it any wonder that NCEA should publish a book dealing with the effects of substance abuse and drug education/prevention?

To think that Catholic school students are not involved with different drugs would be naive. To think that students in elementary schools are not experimenting with drugs would be to reject the evidence. To think that Catholic school educators do not have a responsibility to provide effective educational and prevention programs for their students would be an act of injustice.

Much of the research on drug addiction indicates that such students cut themselves off from other people. One of the strong points of Catholic schools is their rich supportive environment. Every student is valued, every student supports one another and every student models Christian values. Because of this wholesome environment, Catholic schools can assist in a very special way those who are isolated and feel the need to experiment with chemicals.

The Catholic religion provides a strong foundation for seeking "highs" in ways other than through the chemical manipulation of the body. God created people in his own image and likeness. Jesus showed the depth of his love for each person by his suffering and death. And the Spirit of God dwells within each man and woman, boy and girl. For Catholics these are not mere abstract thoughts, these are convictions that affect their every action. Motivated by these beliefs, Catholics have added reasons for refusing to experiment with drugs which will affect their God-given bodies. These same beliefs lead Catholics to show great concern for those who find the need to use such substances. Teachers in Catholic education have the grave responsibility of guiding their students through the turbulent days of youth when the media and peer pressure exert such powerful influences on the young.

The first three chapters of this publication provide teacher education. Teachers, in order to guide students successfully through the adolescent period, need accurate information about drugs and their effects on the body and mind. Teachers having read these chapters will have a much better understanding of bio/psycho/social aspects of drugs. From this understanding, teachers will then ask what can they do. The next five chapters explain the role of teachers in effective drug education, prevention and assistance programs. In these sections the author acknowledges with deep sensitivity the limitations of teachers in terms of time, training and experience.

The author concludes with two chapters addressed to the entire Catholic community. A challenge is presented to initiate comprehensive programs on the national, regional (diocesan) and local (school) levels. Since parents have a special role in assisting their sons and daughters, the book ends with suggestions directed to them.

The Department of Elementary Schools acknowledges with deep gratitude the work of Frank McCorry who with Christian concern has placed for his fellow educators the whole issue of drug education/prevention in the context of our Catholic religion. Teachers will find this readable and practical text helpful to them in their daily tasks. The Department also expresses gratitude to Jan Weiss who served as first editor of the manuscript and Sister Mary Faber, OSF, of Sylvania, Ohio, who proofread the manuscript and composed the index.

The Department offers the book to all the members of the association with the hope that Catholic educators by taking decisive stands on substance abuse, providing effective education and prevention programs to students and showing real concern for those youths involved with drugs will continue to model for the world what is truly effective education.

Robert J. Kealey, Ed.D.   Bonnie Pryor, M.A.
Executive Director   President
         Department of Elementary Schools
      National Catholic Educational Association
                  April 1, 1990

CHAPTER 1: UNDERSTANDING THE PROBLEM

INTRODUCTION

A cartoon recently made the rounds of substance abuse prevention circles that added a certain historical perspective to the problem of youthful substance abuse. The picture featured a forlorn Adam and Eve leaving the Garden of Eden with heads bowed and shoulders sagging. A large hand protruded from the clouds and pointed to the gates of paradise. A serpent observed the scene from a nearby tree. In the caption Eve explained to Adam, "How was I supposed to know the apple was a controlled substance?"

People have always sought something different through the use of controlled substances. Self-knowledge, euphoria, relief from anxiety or depression, increased sexual prowess - the reasons for use are as varied as the individuals using them. Since the 1960's, a growing number of people have used and abused psychoactive substances. As the using group has become more diverse, so has the range and type of psychoactive substances expanded and diversified. The trend has been toward using more powerful mood-altering chemicals with smaller margins of safety. More potent strains of marijuana, reformatted drugs with increased potential for addiction such as Crack, and new synthetic drugs like PCP and other designer drugs have made the already dangerous practice of drug use even more life-threatening. Unfortunately, the group most vulnerable to the consequences of this expanded pharmacopeia is the group least able to handle it, young people.

Understanding the modern phenomenon of widespread psychoactive substance use, particularly as it relates to adolescents, is no small task. Explanations often sound like latter-day versions of the fabled blind men describing an elephant, each explanation accounting for some piece of an extraordinarily large problem. Peer pressure, personality weaknesses, the nuclear age, poor teaching, parenting, nutrition, and television have all been named as culprits in the drug crisis. The complexity of the problem is reflected in the diversity of its purported causes.

Education has come in for a large share of the blame. Yet educators often feel ill-equipped to intervene in drug problems, or to work with students in preventing them. The drug problem can overwhelm a teacher with limited time and resources. Besides, some teachers reason that the students of today often seem to know more than the adults about drug use.

Whatever the misgivings, there can be no doubt that children need guidance regarding the use of psychoactive drugs. Young people's decisions regarding drug use should never be made in isolation without the facts and the support of the people who care most about them. The question for today's teachers is not whether to get involved in drug prevention but how best to get involved within the confines of a school and its mission. Good teaching now requires it. After all, to leave this decision to chance undermines the entire effort to educate and to inform.

BIO/PSYCHO/SOCIAL MODEL OF ABUSE

As an individual behavior and as a social issue, drug abuse is a complex, complicated phenomenon. While different emphases can be placed on particular causes and consequences, most explanations can be grouped into three categories: biological, psychological, and sociological. The key to understanding substance abuse lies in the interplay of these three dimensions.

For each individual the interplay of the bio/psycho/social factors will be unique and dynamic. The process of identifying the relevance of these factors in an individual's decision about drug use lies at the heart of drug prevention. Like the problem itself, prevention programming is also unique and dynamic.

The bio/psycho/social model of substance abuse provides a framework for acknowledging the extraordinary complexity in understanding, preventing, and treating the problem. Not long ago chemical dependency was viewed solely as a problem of the will, or a defect of character. People with these kinds of problems could only be helped when they wanted to be cured which usually meant they had to hit rock bottom. Often the trip down was very painful for the individuals and their families. Part of that trip for young people almost certainly involved separation from school.

The field of chemical dependency has evolved a great deal since the "we are helpless to stop it" era. Far from helpless, the more we, as educators and as parents, do, and the sooner we do it, the better are the chances for halting the slide into addiction. Substance abuse problems can be prevented but this requires an ongoing, intensive program that recognizes the nature of chemical dependency and the addictive process.

Biological Aspect

The biological sciences, specifically research into the brain and its chemical processes, have advanced our understanding of substance abuse in the past ten years. Just 60 years ago scientists firmly perceived that the basic method of communication among the 100 billion or so neurons in the central nervous system was chemical (Koelle, 1975).

Nerve cells (neurons) communicate with each other by releasing a chemical (neurotransmitter) that traverses the minute gap (synapse) separating the neurons. The chemical then attaches itself to a receptor site specifically configured for it in the second neuron. This alters the neuron's electrical charge, thereby causing it either to fire or to rest. This repeated process, as many as 500 times per second, enables one neuron to communicate with thousands of other neurons in different parts of the brain.

Everything that a person does or thinks or feels results from brain functions and neurotransmitters. Falling in love, remembering your childhood, scratching an itch have neurochemical components. The disruption in the production, synthesis and levels of neurotransmitters in the brain has been linked to mental illnesses such as schizophrenia and depression as well as such debilitating conditions as Parkinson's and Alzheimer's disease (Snyder, 1986).

A brain cannot function properly without maintaining the necessary balance in the levels of neurotransmitters. Psychoactive substances disrupt the production, actions, and processes of the brain's neurotransmitters.

Cocaine use provides a good example of how psychoactive drugs affect the brain's communication system. Cocaine, a powerful stimulant, produces intense euphoria for the user almost immediately after ingesting it. This chemical increases the production of the neurotransmitter dopamine (Mule, 1984). Parts of the dopaminergic pathways run through the limbic system of the brain, which regulates our emotional state, and through parts of the cerebral cortex, which affects our thinking processes. The increased availability of dopamine produces euphoria and a heightened sense of confidence in the user. As the cocaine continues to trick the brain into producing unneeded amounts of this neurotransmitter, the effects begin to change. Over a period of months, the dopamine impairs the cortex's ability to assess and test reality, leading at first to increased suspiciousness and eventually to a full-blown paranoid psychosis.

All psychoactive drugs work in a similar fashion. They increase or decrease the activity of the neurotransmitters in the brain (Ray, 1983). Often over a period of time, the alterations in the brain chemistry produce their own set of problems that were unanticipated and even unrecognized by the user in the initial period of use. The risks attached to psychoactive substance abuse grow with repeated use of these powerful compounds.

Rebound effect—Substance abusers do not like to acknowledge a drug's effects, not even when the high wears off. The manipulation of one's brain chemistry through the use of psychoactive agents leads to a biochemical deficit state (Corry and Cimbolic, 1985). This rebound effect usually occurs in the opposite direction from the initial action of the drug. In the case of alcohol, a depressant, the rebound effect is characterized by feelings of agitation and restlessness. Anyone who has experienced a hangover recognizes this odd combination of restlessness and exhaustion. When alcohol's depressant effects wear off, there is a rebound period of restlessness or hyperstimulation before the body can return to normal functioning. At the same time, since alcohol depresses REM or dream sleep in the brain, the individual is exhausted and anxious (Kissin and Bergleiter, 1974). Paradoxical symptoms are not uncommon in rebound as the body attempts to right itself after a period of drug intoxication.

The rebound effect cannot be avoided by prolonging or mixing highs. The deficit state is cumulative and while it can be postponed by continued use of a drug, it cannot be dispelled. Recovering alcoholics have reported disrupted sleep patterns with intensive and frequent dreaming for as long as two years after their last drink (Kinney and Leaton, 1987).

For young people, the rebound effect is a cause for serious concern because of the dramatic physiological changes they are undergoing and their vulnerability to feelings of unhappiness and restlessness. The rebound from the intoxication can become a powerful motivator for repeated use, since they feel even more different after the high than before. The message can quickly become, "The only time that I really feel like myself is when I'm high." Young people do not realize the consequences of their neurochemical brinkmanship nor can they explain this new found circumstance.

Drug and alcohol users rarely understand the biochemical underpinnings of their practices. A knowledge of the neurochemistry of the human body tends to demystify the process of getting high. Users often attach a magical quality to their drug, as if the feelings and experience are somehow not governed by the laws and processes of biology. There is nothing glamorous, however, about neurochemical manipulation. While the mystique of drug use may dim a bit when the process of getting high is explained, nothing is mystical or magical in self-delusion through chemicals. Knowing the biochemistry puts people in touch with the fact that nothing changes when they get high except some microscopic chemicals found somewhere in their brain.

Research advances in understanding addiction— Breakthroughs in the study of neurotransmitters and their receptor sites have altered our thinking about the crucial role that brain processes and genetic codes play in determining addiction. Endorphins are neurotransmitters that modify both the transmission and experience of pain in the brain (Goldstein, 1978). The discovery of natural painkilling neurotransmitters and specialized sites to receive them gives rise to the question that perhaps deficiencies in the way some people's brains produce, process, or store these neurotransmitters might predispose them to opiate addiction.

Research in the field of alcoholism has established a genetic predisposition to alcoholism among children of alcoholic parents (Goodwin et al., 1973). Other research has pointed to similarities in the way the brain processes alcohol and other drugs such as the opiates heroin and morphine. Does a possible underlying common biological basis exist for all chemical dependencies (Wallace, 1985)?

In light of these breakthroughs in brain research, the biological component of the bio/psycho/social model of substance abuse prevention has expanded from concentration on the effects of drugs to understanding the nature of chemical dependency itself. Prevention efforts that do not incorporate a biochemical orientation fail to take advantage of a new understanding of body chemistry and what it means to be human. Natural processes and chemicals in the brain perform similar functions as psychoactive drugs for people who activate them. In other words, modern biology has given a very old adage a new, technological twist: the keys to happiness lie within people themselves. Research into the workings of the brain is beginning to discover those keys.

A biochemical underpinning to substance abuse prevention identifies the physiological mechanisms which can lead people into difficulties. Understanding these processes is particularly important for certain populations, like the children of alcoholic or drug abusing parents, if they are to assess the risks they face in experimenting with drugs. For the general population, the biological dimension points to the inherent risks of any drug-taking. There is always a cost attached to the use of mood-altering drugs. The cost may at times be small, particularly when the use is infrequent, but it exists nonetheless.

The cost in terms of a biological rebound period extends beyond the subjective experience. It increases dramatically when the rebound is delayed through the continued use of drugs. In some unpredictable instances, the actual costs far outweigh the anticipated costs and benefits, as in the case of the gifted, young, world-class athlete Len Bias, who died of a cocaine overdose despite a reported limited involvement with drugs. The perceived risk/benefit ratio, particularly when the evaluator is young and inexperienced, often discounts the dangers inherent in the behavior.

Psychological Aspects

If the biological dimension of the bio/psycho/social model addresses the "how" of drug abuse, the psychological component examines the "why". Parent and teacher groups most often ask me the questions, "Why do young people who have so much to live for throw it all away through this self-destructive behavior? Can't they see what they are doing to themselves? Why don't they stop?"

To understand why drug abusers cannot (or will not) stop, the question why people begin must first be answered. When substance use is reduced to its most basic elements, certain commonalities exist regardless of the substance or the user. All psychoactive drugs have one factor in common: they change the way users feel about themselves and their environment. The change might go in different directions, from the egocentricity of the stimulated cocaine user to the dissociated ego of the PCP user. The constant, however, is that feelings about themselves and their relationship to their surroundings are altered. Users' internal links to themselves and their external hooks to the world are modified and displaced by a chemically-induced euphoria.

These drugs perform their transformation with effortless immediacy and consistency. However, the consistency works only in the short term. As users come to tolerate the drug and attempt to ward off its negative effects, they spend more and more of their time and money trying to recapture the original euphoria which has been lost because of the tolerance of the body for the drug. The spiral of addiction commences as the drug comes to dominate their lives. Many young people in recovery programs talk with great sadness about their frantic attempts to recapture the high. They try chasing after it, but it always eludes them while constantly demanding their attention.

Youthful drug abusers frequently exhibit rebelliousness and social non-conformity. Young drug users feel the constraints and expectations of the adult world most strongly. Their drug use manifests defiance and a means of relief from the threats of the world. Getting high does not generate good feelings. Getting high keeps them busy when they don't know what else to do. Getting high staves off the responsibilities and difficulties of adolescence. Getting high provides identity at a time when an uncertain young person may be desperately seeking one.

Researchers have added immeasurably to understanding the attitudes and behaviors of young substance abusers. Young drug users have many problems (Jessor, Chase and Donovan, 1980). They place little value on academic success and tolerate a greater degree of deviant behavior than their non-using counterparts. They often display a passive surrender to what they perceive as inevitable failure, given their history and their present circumstances. Their sense of hopelessness hinders them from investing in sobriety or abstinence. Of course, the young would not say hopeless. They would say useless. But underneath the cynical demeanor, their experience is closer to feeling overwhelmed and lacking than bored and disinterested.

Kandel and Faust (1975) noticed a greater willingness on the part of some students to engage in minor delinquent acts as a forerunner of drug use initiation. Their research also identified an attitudinal change regarding drug use. Students who initiated the use of a particular drug stated more favorable attitudes toward that drug (e.g. it is safe; it is not addictive) prior to their initiation than students who did not begin to use.

Many young people in recovery speak about how drugs dispelled their feelings of emptiness and connected them with other people. Bill W., a co-founder of Alcoholics Anonymous, said alcohol dissolved an "invisible curtain" that had always separated him from other people. A drug-induced affiliation transforms the isolation and awkwardness felt by many troubled adolescents. The first rushes of euphoria and camaraderie must seem miraculous to youth who have suffered behind their own invisible curtain.

How can young people with so much to offer hurt themselves so badly? Why don't they stop? Because the

drugs make it better for a time, and there was nothing in them before the drugs that seemed worth preserving. Youth with drug problems are often youth without hope.

The social dimension of the bio/psycho/social model examines the impact of all aspects of the environment in supporting or resisting youthful substance abuse. The three elements of family, peer group and availability of illegal substances in the school or community influence people's decisions to use and the degree of that use.

Family—The family shapes children's attitudes toward mood-altering substances. Some research has indicated that parental attitude toward marijuana use was somewhat predictive of their youngsters'involvement with that particular drug (Kandel, 1982). More basic parental considerations may determine young people's attitudes toward drug use, particularly if their parents don't abuse drugs. Parents' attitudes toward the drugs that they use may have a greater impact on their children. Is drunkenness tolerated in the home? How central is the use of alcohol or other drugs to family celebrations? How are conflicts resolved, feelings expressed and acknowledged, and is a psychoactive substance a lubricant or salve to the process? Working with clergy and religious men and women of different faiths, I have found a fair degree of discomfort in addressing parental use as a means of preventing children's use, particularly as it relates to alcohol. The discomfort arises from cultural and religious mores inherent in their upbringing. For example, in working with the Jewish Alcoholics, Chemically Dependent and Significant Others Foundation (JACS) of New York, a self-help organization for recovering Jewish alcoholics and their families, I learned that alcoholism also carries an additional social stigma for Jews because of both biblical injunctions and historical tradition.

On the other hand, having grown up in an Irish Catholic household, I understand the reluctance on the part of some priests and religious to address parental use. The issue in my childhood was not the question of use but what constituted excessive use. The cultural norm that tolerated drunkenness as long as it did not interfere with the breadwinner's ability to earn a living leaves little room for a discussion of the unseen consequences of this behavior, such as encouraging similar use in children. Since many of the Catholic clergy and religious have grown up with these norms, the consequences of opening a dialogue on such behavior often has more personal risks than most topics.

Is parental use of alcohol, therefore, an inappropriate behavior that places children at risk for future problems with all sorts of drugs? No, but neither should the behavior be ignored. How the parents use drugs (legal substances of course, since the use of illegal drugs always communicates something to children) gives the young people their first experience with this particular adult behavior. Parents who avoid discussions about alcohol use or who deny alcohol-related problems send a powerful message to their children. Clergy and religious educators who inadvertently support the secretiveness and denial compound the danger.

In my work with clergy I came across an Episcopal priest, Father Albert Sam, who has a novel solution to the dilemma of sending wrong messages to children. Father Sam asks his congregation to abide by one simple rule in the use of alcohol at family and church functions: "Appropriate use in appropriate settings in appropriate amounts." When the celebration or event is for a child, such as a confirmation or graduation, nothing should take place at that celebration which could not involve the person of honor. Hence, no alcohol is served. When the celebration is for an adult, alcoholic beverages would be available.

One other family influence on children's attitudes toward drugs and their subsequent initiation into the activity which bears mentioning is older sibling use. For many children their introduction to drugs or alcohol comes not from their circle of friends but from older brothers or sisters. The drugs are in the house because of the older children's use and turning little brothers or sisters on is often viewed as no big deal. Of course, the younger children's reaction may be entirely different from their older siblings. The young children may develop problems from their use which may not be the case of the older children.

Peer Group—The best known fact about substance abuse by young people is the role of the peer group in initiating and supporting the behavior. The single best predictor of drug use by teenagers is use by their peer group. Within the peer group, a best friend's use is most predictive (Kandel, 1982). Researchers have not found any other attribute with the same degree of congruence between young people and their peers as the use of illegal drugs. This phenomenon extends almost down to the substance, where the group norm establishes not just the fact of drug use but the type of drug use as well.

While peer pressure exerts itself on both adolescents and adults, adolescents are particularly vulnerable to their peers' opinion. Erikson (1968) describes the dynamics of the group. The process affects at the same time all members of the group. While one youngster might feel so much more unsure than other members in the group, this same feeling is experienced by all members of the group at different times. This means that no one really directs the process. The fluid nature of the peer process accounts for the group's rigidity on the one hand, in which conformity in matters such as dress and music is paramount, and on the other hand the group's spontaneity, in which new things are tried by the entire group on the spur of the moment. The process has an intrinsic factor of unpredictability because of the unsettled nature of all the participants.

Environment— Two aspects of environment have special impact on the bio/psycho/social model of drug addiction: local norms on the public use of psychoactive drugs and the availability of these substances in the community or school.

The macro approach to drug prevention concentrates on establishing behavioral norms that support non-use and that demonstrate clear-cut consequences for violating those norms (Durell and Bukowski, 1984). The consequences are intended to answer the question, "Why should I take drug use seriously?" Since experimentation with psychoactive substances has become so common among young people, educators and community leaders have become reluctant to establish punitive measures for minor infractions. The rationale for a less restrictive policy held that a substance abuse problem has a better chance of surfacing if tight strictures are not imposed. The trade-off is that an unintentional norm becomes established that drug use within certain limits is not that bad and is tolerated.

The tension between helping those in need and condoning the use of psychoactive drugs needs to be resolved. Success requires a consistent message across systems which interact with young people. Similar norms governing drug use in the school, at the local movie, and at the local concert hall serve to reinforce each other. They underscore behaviorally the basic concept that drug use can be a dangerous practice which has serious consequences. The norms must emphasize genuine consequences for inappropriate behavior, however sanctions do not necessarily have to address the issue of criminality. The suspension of privileges, the cancellation of events, the reduction of programs, the introduction of more restrictive procedures (e.g. locker searching, bag searching before concerts, etc.), communicate the seriousness of infractions. Use of local police in a school that has had recurring incidents of drug dealing on the premises is warranted.

While the establishment of group norms is not an easy task, all groups which interact with children—parents, teachers, clergy, merchants, police—must deliver the same message in order to heighten the chances that the message will be heard and respected.

Availability—When a school or community is awash in drugs, efforts to keep students straight are severely compromised. Good prevention requires good enforcement. While the pressure to use is subtle enough that no one is actually "forced" to use something, availability clearly affects usage levels. Dealers are not menacing figures in trench coats who cackle about enslaving young minds. They are young people who a year before were students and friends. The drug business at the peer level can be very intimate and very seductive. Schools and communities that do not insist on intensive enforcement of the drug laws at the peer level place an unfair burden on young people to reject drug use.

SUMMARY

The placement of the problem of youthful substance abuse in a bio/psycho/social framework allows for a dynamic interpretation of the forces that bear on young people's decisions and practices. Each dimension may dominate in a particular circumstance, setting, or individual. More often the factors interact to fashion a unique set of circumstances facing a particular individual, school or community. The bio/psycho/social model allows that the reasons for use can be as varied as the people using the drugs. Understanding the mix of factors at work in my school, my community, my family, or even myself is a first step in developing a response to the issue.

An inventory of a school's program from a bio/psycho/social perspective may reveal needs that have not yet been addressed.

How responsive is the program in identifying and working with at risk populations like the children of alcoholic parents?

How effective is the program in breaking through the isolation that is so characteristic of early adolescence and in making use of the peer dynamic in organizing and renewing program strategies?

How well has the school reached outside itself to develop a consistent message throughout the community?

What should be done to remedy the weaknesses at a classroom and a policy level?

The implications of the bio/psycho/social model shall be explained in later chapters, first in terms of the drugs of initiation for young people and then in terms of a comprehensive approach to prevention.

13

REFERENCES:

Corry, J.M. & Cimbolic, P. (1985). *Drugs: Facts, Alternatives, Decisions.* Belmont, CA: Wadsworth Publishing Co.

Durrell, J. & Bukowski, W. (1884). Preventing substance abuse: The state of the art. *Public Health Report, 99,* 23-31.

Erikson, E. (1968). *Identity: Youth and Crisis.* New York: Norton.

Goldstein, A. (1978). Endorphins. *The Sciences, 18* (3).

Goodwin, D.W., Schulsinger, F., Hermansen, L., Guze, S.B., & Winoken, G. (1973). Alcohol problems in adoptees raised apart from their alcoholic biological parents. *Archives of General Psychiatry, 28,* 238-243.

Jessor, R., Chase, J. A., & Donovan, J. E. (1980). Psychosocial correlates of marijuana use and problem drinking in a national sample of adolescents. *American Journal of Public Health, 70,* 604-613.

Kandel D. (1982). Inter- and intra-generational influences on adolescent marijuana use. *Journal of the American Academy of Child Psychiatry, 21,* 328-347.

_____ & Faust, R. (1975). Sequences and stages in patterns of adolescent drug use. *Archives of General Psychiatry, 32,* 923-932.

Kinney, J. & Leaton, G. (1987). *Loosening the Grip* (3rd ed.). St. Louis: Times Mirror/Mosby College Publishing.

Kissin B. & Bergleiter, H. (Eds.) 1974. *The Biology of Alcoholism* (Vols. 1-2). New York: Plenum Press.

Koelle, G.B. (1975). Neurohumoral transmission and the autonomic nervous system. Goodman, L.S. & Gilman, A. (Eds.) *The Pharmacological Basis of Therapeutics.* New York: MacMillan.

Mule, S. (1984). The pharmacodynamics of cocaine abuse. *Psychiatric Annals, 14,* 724-727.

Ray, O. (1983). *Drugs, Society and Human Behavior* (3rd ed.). St. Louis: Mosby.

Snyder, S.H. (1986). *Drugs and the Brain.* New York: Scientific American Books.

Wallace, J. (1985). *Alcoholism: New Light on the Disease.* Salisbury, N.C.: Lexis Press.

CHAPTER 2:
GATEWAY DRUGS:
THE BEGINNING OF
THE PROBLEM

INTRODUCTION

The bio/psycho/social model of substance use assumes that all psychoactive substance use contains risks. Users may decide that the cost/benefit ratio favors their usage (Johnson, 1980). Nevertheless, such factors as rebound, the self-reinforcing qualities of psychoactive drugs, and the addictive potential of some drugs invite real danger. Escalation of those costs directly relates to personal, developmental and situational factors which make some individuals more vulnerable to drug use. In fact, most adolescents who experiment with addictive substances do not develop immediate problems. Because of the volatile nature of adolescence, however, seemingly trouble-free use is a fluid rather than static condition. The essential element in developing a problem with psychoactive drugs is to use them. Heightened vulnerability gives greater force to this innocuous pre-condition.

The bio/psycho/social model does not support the assumption that certain drugs are okay to use and other drugs are bad to use. The "good drug, bad drug" hypothesis frequently an unstated personal conviction may be stated as, "The drugs that I use are good, the drugs that other people use are bad. That is why they have drug problems." The corollary of the "good drug, bad drug" hypothesis is the postulate of abuse which states that abuse of a drug begins just beyond the limits of one's own personal practice. "I have my use of drugs completely under control. I only use good drugs and I use them in a very responsible manner." Outside of these parameters lies the danger zone which exists for everyone else but not for this person.

Legal drugs do not necessarily mean good (safe) drugs. Alcohol users may cite its legality to reinforce the appropriateness of their behavior which is not illegal behavior such as smoking marijuana. Conversely, marijuana smokers continually recite the dangers of alcohol and the purported fewer dangers of marijuana.

Legal or illegal, popular or uncommon, infrequently or regularly used, drugs which affect the brain's chemistry have dangerous potential. They each have associated with their use physical and emotional costs which escalate with continued use. Information about substance abuse must underscore that the entire spectrum of psychoactive substances can present problems to their users. The body and psyche make no legal or other distinctions in their response to the chemical.

Prevention strategies at the elementary and middle school levels initially focus on drugs that can be legally used by adult members of our society: nicotine and alcohol (Polich et al., 1984). Children begin their substance use careers with legal drugs before moving on to the illegal drugs like marijuana (Kandel, 1978). Success in preventing or delaying the use of gateway drugs can make the difference between experimental use and problematic use in children's future.

This chapter focuses on some of the bio/psycho/social aspects of gateway drugs - drugs that introduce the user to the practice and effects of mood-altering chemicals (DuPont, 1984). A comprehensive review of all the facts and dangers of these powerful compounds can be found in texts devoted to the examination of each of the gateway drugs. This chapter examines these drugs within a bio/psycho/social framework and relates that framework to a substance abuse prevention setting.

NICOTINE

Who doesn't remember their first cigarette, the circumstances, the people, the setting? For me, smoking tobacco began on a Friday evening after a dance when I was in the eighth grade. The memory of the experience, of the sense of independence and bravado and of being young and out on a Friday night still lingers in my mind. I can remember the promise that the night held for me. Nights had always been the time that ended play, the time to be indoors awaiting the new day. That night found me on my own, and for the first time realizing it. Walking down Crosby Avenue in the Pelham Bay section of the Bronx surrounded by 10 or 20 close personal friends was heady stuff. It would not be ruined by any failure on my part to assert my independence and maturity by not smoking. Smoking only seemed to affirm it.

I carried the legacy of that special night in the form of a nicotine addiction for the next twenty years of my life. Of course, if someone had tried to warn me of my dangerous flirtation with a highly addictive substance, I would not have listened. The social norm supported the behavior, and I was not about to be caught being anything less than hip on that Friday long ago. Nicotine is a highly addictive chemical that kept bringing me back for more smokes even after the thrill was gone.

Nicotine, a highly addictive stimulant mimics the action of the neurotransmitter acetylcholine in the brain (Julien, 1981). Acetylcholine affects muscle tone and the involuntary mechanisms in the brainstem like breathing. Nicotine also increases the production of epinephrine in the adrenal gland. Nicotine raises the brain's arousal level and prepares the body for the flight or fight response. Blood pressure, heart rate, muscle tone all increase (Sieden and Dykstra, 1977).

While the heart has increased demands placed on it by the heightened arousal state, the availability of oxygen decreases. Carbon monoxide in the tobacco smoke binds more effectively to the hemoglobin in the blood, which leaves little room for oxygen to be transported to an excited heart (Schlaadt and Shannon, 1986). Increased work for the heart without the necessary fuel can result in a cardiac disaster. Since tobacco smoke damages the lungs it further reduces the volume of oxygen available for healthy functioning of the body.

Smoking and cancer are inextricably linked. Lung, esophagal, pancreatic and bladder cancers exist more often among smokers than non-smokers. Respiratory ailments like emphysema, bronchitis, asthma and cardiovascular diseases exist more often among smokers than non-smokers (U. S. Department of Health and Human Services, 1982). In short, smoking is just about the worst single behavior anyone can do for one's health.

Nicotine consumption also produces psychological effects which are mild compared to other psychoactive drugs. Some smokers report after smoking a heightened sense of well-being, higher mental acuity, greater concentration on details, and a greater sense of purpose to their efforts. These "benefits" result from the heightened arousal level produced by the stimulant nicotine. Other smokers, however, report a more calming effect, a pleasurable unwinding. Dose-related problems may occur when a smoker can't calm down after smoking too many cigarettes in too short a period of time. Heart racing, restlessness, and a feeling of being out of control are some of the unpleasant effects of a tobacco overdose. These may pass quickly by lowering the nicotine level in the blood through a short period of abstinence (Julien, 1981).

Smoking takes on a special lustre in the arena of social interactions. Young people assume this behavior as an accoutrement of their adult status. The belief that one can stop anytime runs contrary to the evidence. In this regard smoking does not differ from alcoholism and other forms of substance abuse. The "I can stop anytime" mentality is a delusion not limited to the young or to nicotine addiction.

Although attitudes toward smoking have undergone a radical change in the past twenty years, the behavior still holds great attraction for young people. Perhaps this change in attitudes causes an even greater allure for some young people. As smoking becomes increasingly identified as harmful and destructive to the body, its practice has taken on a harder edge. Smoking is no longer considered a benign, transitional behavior to adult status. Smoking now has an added element of defiance and rebelliousness. Tobacco smoking may be taking on some of the symbolism that marijuana smoking held for a previous generation.

ALCOHOL

Alcohol is the quintessential adult beverage in social situations. Approximately 110 million alcohol users in

America consume approximately six billion gallons of alcoholic beverages per year. In 1982 this amount equaled 320 cans (12 ozs.) of beer, 12.5 fifths of wine, and 10.5 quarts of distilled spirits for every American 14 years or older, or two drinks per day for every American over the age of 13 (Califano, 1983).

Alcohol problems would be less severe if Dr. Anstie's limit of two drinks per day (Cohen, 1983), first prescribed in the nineteenth century, was observed. However consumption rates vary greatly. Eleven million (10%) of the alcohol users consume 50% of all alcohol products. An estimated 13 million alcoholic or problem drinkers live in America. Three million of the alcohol abusers are adolescents.

Alcohol is embedded in our cultural consciousness as the requisite celebratory potion for all occasions. Our professional athletes douse each other in it and swig from foaming bottles while granting post-game interviews. It heralds hundreds of occasions and life events from winning a national election to the TGIF celebration. Can you visualize an adult social setting where alcohol is not a welcomed guest? Its use is a common and, if the truth be told, for the most part positive experience for people. No other drug, however, has caused as much harm and pain to people as alcohol.

Alcohol is the central drug experience for many young people. Even for those who move beyond the exclusive use of alcohol to other psychoactive drugs, their alcohol use continues. Alcohol remains enormously popular, relatively cheap and widely available. Given these facts, any substance abuse prevention program must address the use of alcohol by young people.

Biological Aspects

Although classified as a central nervous system depressant, the biochemistry of alcohol is extraordinarily complex and still not fully understood. No doubt exists on the drug's depressive effects at both the cellular and systemic levels of the brain. Alcohol's effects on the brain systems result in a subjective state of both stimulation and disinhibition when taken in small doses. How alcohol creates this mixed effect in the brain is not well understood.

The drug demonstrates a remarkable diversity in exerting its action on neurons, and no completely acceptable theory to explain alcohol's effects on the brain exists (Berry and Pentreath, 1980). Despite these limitations, what is known is chilling: alcohol is toxic, destroys brain cells, and affects every body organ and system which uses energy (Kinney and Leaton, 1987).

The first metabolite created by the liver's breakdown of the drug alcohol for eventual excretion as carbon dioxide and water is a substance known as acetaldehyde. Acetaldehyde is highly toxic and is quickly broken down by liver enzymes. However when acetaldehyde interacts with certain neurotransmitters, it produces a whole series of substances, tetrahydroisoquinolines or TIQ's, which have been shown in the laboratory to have enormous effects on the drinking habits of laboratory animals. Meyers (1978) has shown that the presence of TIQ's in the brains of monkeys leads to an irreversible preference for alcohol over water (monkeys normally loathe alcohol).

TIQ's have also been shown to bind at the same receptor sites in the brain as one of the endorphins and the addictive drug morphine (heroin and codeine as well). Is there a common link in the way the brain processes these substances? The question is only now being investigated. However, Wallace (1985) has noted that the brain of the alcoholic treats alcohol in much the same way as heroin that an addict shoots directly into the veins.

Genetic Predisposition

The past twenty years have witnessed a steady and impressive stream of findings on the essential role of genetics in the development of alcoholism. Little doubt exists that an alcoholic parent is the single best predictor of alcoholism in an individual. Goodwin (1988), in his historic studies of adopted children whose biological parents were alcoholic but who were raised by adoptive non-alcoholic parents, discovered that the sons of alcoholics were four times more likely to be alcoholics than the sons of non-alcoholic parents. His research further suggested that being raised in an alcoholic home was less predictive of alcoholism than being the child of an alcoholic. Vaillant's (1983) longitudinal study of subjects from adolescence through adulthood discovered the same phenomenon.

Studies have shown that alcoholics and non-alcoholics handle this drug's effects differently (Goodwin, 1985). Alcoholics can drink more, experience the drug's effects more intensely, and suffer fewer dysphoric effects from drinking than non-alcoholics, particularly early in their drinking history. The rate at which the body eliminates alcohol is almost totally inherited. Children of an alcoholic parent eliminate alcohol more quickly than children of non-alcoholic parents, thereby avoiding some of the negative short term effects of alcohol abuse which may diminish interest in repeated use (Murray and Gurling, 1980).

While scientists do not completely understand this genetic predisposition, they know one gene or site is not totally responsible. However, the conclusion to be derived from this field of research remains unequivocal: children of an alcoholic parent are at greater risk for alcoholism regardless of their environment. When recovering alcoholics speak about being alcoholic since birth, they may be expressing a basic biological truth.

Young people beginning their use of psychoactive drugs rarely understand that for some of them the game is fixed and the deck is loaded. Everyone in the Friday night beer group does not take the same risks. Given the developmental issues of pre-adolescence and adolescence, alcohol use tends to reinforce itself because of the psychological and social relief experienced under its influence. Those rewards can impel youngsters toward frighteningly regular abuse of this dangerous drug. For young people with the added factor of heightened biogenetic risk, the allure can be almost irresistible. The trifecta of developmental curiosity, psycho/social benefits, and genetic predisposition will spell disaster for them once drinking is initiated.

Psychological Aspects

Most educators know the psychological effects of alcohol abuse among adolescents. Alcohol bolsters an immature ego so that the person bristles (or staggers) with confidence and disinhibition. Unfortunately, teenagers grow to maturity only through the fire storm of experience called

21

adolescence. Regular alcohol use robs individuals of opportunities to confront the anxieties characteristic of the age and to seek solutions. The development of such youth is arrested in the pseudo-adulthood of adolescence. The effects of this arrested development reverberate throughout their lives as these youngsters fail to meet the challenges of adulthood (Erikson, 1968).

Reliance on alcohol breeds further reliance on alcohol as a means of coping. The earlier the person begins to rely on alcohol to cope, to socialize, to be recognized, the more difficulty a person has in overcoming this reliance.

Because young people generally enjoy the excitement of new experiences, especially those with an element of risk in them, each acute episode of alcohol use presents serious but unanticipated dangers. Alcohol's disinhibiting effects create in users a diminished capacity for good judgment. Combined with the adolescent's inexperience in assessing personal risks, these new experiences can be disastrous. Criminal behavior, acts of delinquency, assaultive behavior, unwanted pregnancies, speeding, and fatal auto accidents often have an alcohol component to their occurrence. The clear relationship between alcohol and teenage sexual behavior is particularly disturbing. Some young people may not have bargained for the consequences of cutting loose when high, nor did they anticipate their diminished capacity for good judgment when intoxicated.

The need for stimulation, the unsanctioned outlet for aggression, and the anti-authoritarian nature of teenage drinking provide insights into understanding their behavior. Drug use becomes both the means and the channel for the expression of risk-taking and rebellious activity. Moreover, under the influence of the drug youngsters may experiment with other adult behaviors which have their own sets of dangers and consequences. Substance abuse prevention programming, particularly for adolescents, must make room for the rebellious nature of adolescence, and strive to be creative enough that young people can take some risks and stretch their wings through their participation.

Sociological Aspects

American society spends two billion dollars per year on alcohol advertising. One cannot open a magazine or watch a television show without observing several commercials enticing the viewer or reader to imbibe. While most people view drinking alcoholic beverages as acceptable adult behavior, a clear trend of intolerance for inappropriate and excessive drinking has emerged. This dramatic shift in leniency toward drunk drivers represents a revolution in the attitudes of Americans. Mothers Against Drunk Driving (MADD) and similar groups have highlighted the deadly dangers of drunk driving and have caused state legislatures to toughen their stance against what had previously been an accepted practice.

Adolescents experiment with alcohol in social situations. The social situation brings together a group of friends where everyone observes everyone. Individual teen performance heightens or lowers that youth's status in a number of social networks. Not drinking, and unfortunately, not drinking enough may earn the adolescent the reputation of not being cool and no teenager wishes this designation. The maelstrom of conflicting feelings about what the young person actually wants to do and what is perceived as necessary to maintain status in the group creates an environment for potential trouble and anxiety. The prevention-oriented group helps individuals to recognize, express, and resolve these dilemmas. Encouraging students to face these problems results in less drinking and greater success in abuse prevention.

The advertising industry complicates young people's struggles to arrive at thoughtful decisions regarding the use of alcohol because the advertisements have equated the use of alcohol with youthful exuberance, good looks and sophistication. The adaptation of successful rock and roll songs and the use of innovative upbeat or sultry visual displays reinforce the idea that drinking is cool. Such advertising denies the realities of alcohol abuse among teenagers.

MARIJUANA

Discussions about the relative safety of marijuana use have become more muted in recent years. However, the contention remains that marijuana is a relatively benign substance if used in moderation. Some will even say that marijuana, while illegal, is safer than the legal drug alcohol. The marijuana/alcohol debate exemplifies the "good drug/ bad drug" dispute described in Chapter 1. This approach ignores the underlying risks inherent in the acute use of all psychoactive compounds.

Biological Aspects

Current research into the deleterious effects of marijuana has begun to build a case for avoiding the drug altogether, much in the same way that previous research efforts into tobacco smoking slowly demonstrated its enormous health and social costs. The respiratory damage caused by the regular deposit of the tars found in marijuana smoke on the lungs equals and possibly exceeds the damage done by cigarette smoking. Marijuana smoke contains the same carcinogens found in tobacco smoke and produces 50% more tar than a strong commercial brand of tobacco (MacDonald, 1980).

Marijuana clearly interferes with short term memory processes in the brain and impairs motor coordination and reaction time which make driving under the drug's influence a hazardous and reckless activity. Marijuana impairs the body's immune system, lowering its resistance to viruses and infections through depression of T-lymphocyte helper cells (Institute of Medicine, 1982).

Marijuana's depressive effects on brain activity and the effects of chronic use on reproductive functions require further investigation. The field of marijuana research is only now emerging from its infancy. Of the 421 known chemicals in the marijuana plant, 60 are cannabinoids, i.e., pharmacologically active chemicals occurring only in the marijuana plant. Many of these have yet to be identified and investigated (MacDonald, 1980).

Basic research into the actions of the drug's principal psychoactive ingredient, delta-9 tetrahydrocannabinol or THC, identified a wide range of benefits and potential dangers. The research has raised more alarms and cautions than were previously recognized. Compelling answers to complex research questions such as the effect of the storage of THC in body fat on brain and organ functions, the neurochemical effects and deficits of regular marijuana use, and the long term behavioral effects of marijuana use will ultimately reveal the full range of risk in the behavior. Current knowledge, however, clearly demonstrates that marijuana is neither safe nor benign. Its use has potentially serious consequences for people's health and well-being. Future research will only validate how dangerous those consequences really are.

Psychological Aspects

Marijuana's efficiency in easing the psychological and social demands of growing up make it especially attractive to vulnerable youth (Labouvie, 1980). The marijuana high slows things down, softens the edges of reality, and makes the most insignificant detail enormously interesting and engrossing. By interfering with the brain's normal ability to sort out irrelevant stimuli, the marijuana high gives young persons the illusion of a more direct, immediate experience of self and their environment (Tinklenburg and Dorley, 1976). Everything appears richer, more alive, and more present. Startling insights into music and people and self may occur. The marijuana high enables one to be, to be in the present without doubt and worry. Marijuana poses the real danger of quelling the normal but necessary fears which characterize all youth's progress to adulthood.

The ambivalence that dominates young people's struggles to answer the most basic question of selfhood, "Who am I?" reverberates through the entire experience of adolescence. A lack of understanding and appreciation of themselves creates uncertainty in how to feel about things, what they really like to do and what matters most. Youngsters' doubts can dominate and deplete their emotional energy. Doubt leads to anxiety, anxiety further immobilizes, teenagers feel lost and adrift among those who appear so confident and assured. In this struggle youth fluctuate between boredom and tedium. If only something would happen, anything to break the monotony of adolescent existence, goes the reasoning, things would be better.

138, 193 **College of St. Francis Librar**
Joliet, Illinois

Enter marijuana. Not only does the drug quiet the fears and make youngsters' internal experiences more vibrant, but the effects seem to be undetectable to parents and teachers. Since such students present no trouble in the classroom, teachers may not perceive a need. After all, other challenges exist in the classroom with the more provocative and disruptive students. If some students seem out of it every once in a while, so does every other youngster from time to time.

At home, these children appear more withdrawn and less open, but present no major problems. The group of friends may have changed, the teens may be moodier and less tolerant of siblings and parental intrusions, but again, that is the nature of the age. Parents may reason, "If I can't be flexible and adapt to the changes my child shows during this turbulent period, I will drive myself crazy and won't be of any use when a real need appears."

The insidious process that leads to troubled, dysfunctional drug use poses the real danger to youth who use marijuana. This drug quietly erodes individuals' interest in the world. Things go better with pot, it's as simple as that. In fact things aren't going anywhere. Such teenagers stagnate and growth in self-knowledge is retarded. Because the drug provides a supposed more immediate and pleasant experience, youth vehemently resist any suggestion of losing whatever tentative sense of self they have developed. Eventually these teens become more fragmented and less responsive to personal needs.

In the initial stages of use, parents and teachers may fail to recognize the subtle changes in their students' communication and openness. Unconsciously such individuals come to rely on the drug to resolve doubts, boredom, and the anxiety of their former life. In fact, adolescents reject the opportunity to work through their feelings of alienation, isolation, and boredom to a healthy maturity. Marijuana becomes the all-encompassing solution for all problems and difficulties.

Sociological Aspects

Marijuana use not only changes the internal frame of reference for students, but it also provides a social network and the means to hold it together. Marijuana smoking takes place in groups, becomes a core activity and creates the group's identity. Kandel (1985) has documented the group as a dynamic influence in the decision to smoke pot. The camaraderie and the affiliation express the unacknowledged but central fact for adolescents in trouble with pot: marijuana answers all their questions.

REFERENCES

Berry, M. & Pentreath, V. W. (1980). The neurophysiology of alcohol. In M. Sandler (Ed.), *The Psychopharmacology of Alcohol.* New York: Raven Press.

Califano, J. (1983). *The 1982 Report of Drug Abuse and Alcoholism.* New York: Warner Books.

Cohen, S. (1983). *The Alcoholism Problems.* New York: Haworth Press.

Dupont, R.L. (1984). *Getting Tough on Gateway Drugs.* Washington, DC: American Psychiatric Press.

Erickson, E. (1968). *Identity: Youth and Crisis.* New York: Norton.

Goodwin, D. (1985). Alcoholism and Genetics. *Archives of General Psychiatry, 42,* 171-174.

(1988). *Is Alcoholism Hereditary?* New York: Ballantine.

Institute of Medicine (1982). *Marijuana and Health.* Washington, DC: National Academy.

Johnson, V. (1980). *I'll Quit Tomorrow.* New York: Harper and Row.

Julien, R.M. (1981). *A Primer of Drug Action* (3rd ed.). San Francisco: W.H. Freeman and Sons.

Kandel, D. (Ed.) (1978). *Longitudinal Research on Drug Use: Empirical Findings and Methodological Issues.* Washington, DC: Hemisphere-Wiley.

_____ (1985). On processes of peer influences in adolescent drug use: A developmental perspective. *Alcohol and Substance Abuse in Adolescence.* 139-161.

Kinney, J. & Leaton, G. (1987). *Loosening the Grip.* St. Louis: C.V. Mosby.

Labouvie, E. (1980). Alcohol and marijuana use in relation to adolescent stress. *The International Journal of the Addictions, 21,* 333-345.

MacDonald, J. (1980). Cannabis: Adverse effects on health. *Journal of the Addiction Research Foundation of Ontario,* January.

Meyers, R.D. (1978). Tetrahydroisoquinolines in the brain: The basis of an animal model of alcoholism. *Alcoholism Experimental Research, 2,* 145-154.

Murray, R.M., & Gurling, H.M. (1980). Genetic contributions to normal and abnormal drinking. In M. Sandler (Ed.). *The Psychopharmacology of Alcohol.* New York: Raven Press.

Polich, J.M., Ellickson, P. L., Reuter, P. & Kahan, J.P. (1984). *Strategies for Controlling Adolescent Drug Use.* Santa Monica: The Rand Corporation.

Schlaadt, R.G. & Shannon, P. T. (1986). *Drugs of Choice* (2nd ed.). Englewood: Prentice Hall.

Sieden, L.S. & Dykstra. L.A. (1977). *Psychopharmacology: A Biochemical and Behavioral Approach.* New York: Van Nostrand Reinhold.

Tinklenburg, J.R. & Dorley, C. F. (1976). A model of marijuana's cognitive effects. In Brande, J. & Szara, T. (Eds.). *Pharmacology of Marijuana.* New York: Raven Press.

U.S. Department of Health and Human Services, (1982). *The Health Consequences of Smoking: Cancer.* Washington: U. S. Government Printing Office.

Vaillant, G.E. (1983). *The Natural History of Alcoholism: Causes, Patterns and Paths to Recovery.* Cambridge: Harvard University Press.

Wallace, J. (1985). *Alcoholism: New Light on the Disease.* Salisbury, NC: Lexis Press.

CHAPTER 3:
COCAINE, CRACK, DESIGNER DRUGS

INTRODUCTION

In the not so distant future a doctoral student will write a dissertation on the phenomenon of crack use in our society. The study will not be in psychology or sociology, but in economics or marketing, because the crack story is first and foremost a story about business. The crack phenomenon presents a textbook case of repackaging a product to suit consumer needs and to ensure consumer loyalty. The story needs to be told because of its dangerous implications for the future. Crack has raised the stakes in the drug game that many young people play on their way to adulthood, and like most games of chance, the odds are stacked against the players.

Crack is a smokeable, highly addictive form of the stimulant drug cocaine. It is reformatted cocaine. Cocaine, a highly unstable alkaloid of the coca plant, loses its potency very quickly once removed from the bush (Mule, 1984). In order to preserve its potency for transportation and eventual sale, cocaine is chemically bonded to a hydrochloric salt. Cocaine hydrochloride, a white, powdery substance, became increasingly popular throughout all levels of society in the 1970's and 80's.

COCAINE

The cocaine hydrochloride sold on the streets of America contains approximately 25% cocaine and 75% adulterants like mannitol and lactose which added to the coke increase its bulk, thereby its profitability (Cohen, 1984). Cocaine hydrochloride, most commonly snorted through the nose, becomes absorbed by the mucous membranes in the nose, enters the blood stream, and within a minute's time arrives at the brain to produce the neurochemical effects of cocaine euphoria. The high lasts approximately 30 minutes. The depressive rebound effect reinforces the desire to use cocaine again. Continued use leads to an intense dependency and an overwhelming desire to use the drug repeatedly. With chronic use over a period of time, the drug comes to dominate the person's life. Some people have lost everything in the pursuit of cocaine - their self-respect, their families, their professions, and even their lives.

The cocaine high has been described as an intensely powerful, orgasmic experience. In laboratory studies with monkeys, unlimited access to cocaine led to the animals' rejection of such basic life sustaining necessities as food and water in favor of cocaine (Aigner and Balster, 1978). A monkey would arouse itself from cocaine-induced seizures, and immediately return to the cocaine-dispensing lever for more of the same. Cocaine is that powerful a reinforcer. Recovering cocaine addicts describe similar effects. No matter what amount of cocaine was available, it would be consumed and still not satiate their cocaine compulsion. The cocaine addict never has enough.

FREEBASING

Cocaine aficionados soon tired of the 25% cocaine high, since tolerance to the drug's euphoric effects does develop. In their search for ever better ways to reach the heights of cocaine euphoria, people began to freebase their cocaine.

The freebasing process frees the cocaine from its hydrochloride base so that only cocaine, 90% to 100% cocaine, is delivered to the brain at one time. Freebasing breaks the chemical bond that holds the cocaine to the hydrochloride salt by means of the volatile gas ether and heat. This practice is dangerous in the best of circumstances. However, after hours or even days of a cocaine binge, when the person experiences the nervous hyperstimulation of cocaine intoxication, freebasing can be downright foolhardy. Richard Pryor, the actor-comedian, exemplified the dangers of cocaine freebasing, he almost burned himself to death while freebasing.

The intricate and dangerous process of freebasing limited its appeal, so that freebasing never became a dominant method of cocaine use. Treatment professionals observed how quickly smoking freebased cocaine resulted in addiction and dysfunction when compared with snorting cocaine hydrochloride. The dangerous practice remained among a relatively small group of heavy cocaine abusers. In 1984 on the streets of New York City, crack appeared and changed the rules for many cocaine users.

CRACK

Crack, free-based cocaine, requires neither the use of ether nor the skill of a chemist to prepare. It is smokeable, 85% to 95% cocaine, and delivers the same bang to the brain as freebase. It can be (and is) brewed in the average kitchen with a blender, some baking soda, water, and heat. The baking soda serves the same catalytic function as ether in breaking the chemical bonds present in cocaine hydrochloride (Hall, 1986). Cocaine is blended with baking soda and water, heated until all that remains is a flat pancake of white, beige, or grey color, dried until hard, broken into small chunks, placed in clear plastic vials with color-coded caps, and sold on the street for as little as five dollars per vial. With this simple transformation, the dangerous substance cocaine becomes deadly.

When speaking to parents' groups I make a special effort to describe the crack high so that they understand its attractiveness as well as its dangers. I describe the high usually by portraying a salesperson addressing a group of parents.

Thank you, ladies and gentlemen, for your invitation to speak here this evening. I have a special interest in parent-child relations and in assisting parents to feel good about themselves, their spouse and their children. I understand the pressures that parents have today, the incredible stress and tension that is a part of modern living. There is no more difficult job, in my opinion, than raising children today. You can often feel depressed and uncertain about your efforts. You might question your own abilities, and feel bad about yourself in the process. I know that you can feel awfully tired at the end of a day of managing the many demands on your time and person, leaving no time for yourself and maybe even diminished interest in your family. Being tired and unsure can sometimes feel like a way of life rather than a temporary condition.

That's why I asked to talk to you tonight. I have developed a product that will ease those burdens. You will feel confident in yourself; in fact you will be on top of the world. You will feel surer of your own abilities and direction. You will have more energy, need less sleep, and no longer feel tired or depressed. While this program is a stress-reduction program, one of the great side-benefits is that you will lose weight (as much as 20 pounds per month) effortlessly and quickly without feeling hungry or dieting. Truth in advertising, however, compels me to tell you that the down side of the program is that you will like how you feel so much, that you will want to feel this way all the time. This product has been priced so that even people of moderate means can use it. It is only $5 or $10 per unit. I will be taking orders out by my car and shall return nightly to see how everyone is doing. Cash, please, no checks, credit cards nor credit.

Thank you for your attention.

My sales pitch has described the initial experiences of a crack high and the powerful psychological needs that crack seems to meet.

Crack, as it is smoked, enters the already oxygenated blood through the lungs and arrives at the brain in a matter of three to five seconds (Brenner and Kostant, 1986). Because of the greater surface area of the lungs in comparison to the mucous membranes in the nose, the volume of the drug immediately available to the brain is much greater. The potency of the material, the volume available, and the route of administration create an immediate, intense and dramatic shift in the brain's functioning and the individual's perception of self and the environment.

Biological Aspects

Crack and cocaine share the same bio/psycho/social effects. The crack user experiences the effects more intensely and these effects cause enormous problems more quickly, but crack does nothing differently from cocaine. Blood pressure, heart rate, temperature and respiration all elevate. The body produces more adrenalin as it prepares itself for the atavistic fight or flight response. Surface blood vessels close, the blood flows to the musculature, and digestion slows or stops. At the same time, the drug cocaine allows the neurotransmitter norepinephrine to have a heightened effect by prolonging its action in the brainstem and the motor and judgment centers of the cerebral cortex (Verebrey and Gold, 1980). The overall effect includes hyperarousal, enhanced mental acuity, sharpened sensory response and feelings of dominance and competence. Cocaine - crack - is a "can-do" drug.

Cocaine also affects the neurotransmitter dopamine. Besides its action on motor and judgement functions, dopamine is a major neurotransmitter in the pleasures centers of the brain, which reside in the limbic system that borders the midbrain. The limbic system adds the emotional content to experience. The intense euphoria, the sexual stimulation, and the feelings of well-being can be traced to cocaine's action on dopamine and norepinephrine levels in the limbic system (Wise, 1984).

Crack Rebound

People rebound from crack in as powerful a manner as the high was intense. Immediately following the short-lived high (only 5 to 10 minutes in duration), users experience a deficit state of lethargy, discomfort, anxiety, and even mild depression that contrasts markedly with the euphoria just experienced. In my conversations with young people in treatment for crack abuse, a number of them recounted their immediate reaction to their initial crack use with the words, "Man, I gotta do that again!"

Crack, even in the initial experiences, provides a powerful reinforcer that compels the user to continue use. Repeated use quickly enhances the deficit state to a severe depression that users describe as all consuming. As the crack high loses some of its lustre, an intense, uncontrollable compulsion to use and a desire to avoid the crash replace the euphoria. Excess dopamine levels in the brain result in severe paranoia. The body in its state of hyperstimulated overdrive consumes itself as the person loses drastic amounts of weight. The neurotransmitter serotonin which mediates sleep and our more primitive, impulsive rage centers stops being produced, placing the user on a hair trigger for violence. Impotence, frigidity, and a disinterest in sex complete the transformation (Gold, Washton, and Dackis, 1985). In as short a period as six months, experimental use can escalate to chronic abuse. The crack addict becomes a paranoid, hostile, potentially violent individual driven to repeat the practice that has placed the individual in such a condition.

When the crack user ends his run, usually because there is no more crack, no more money, and complete exhaustion, a tremendously uncomfortable crash occurs. An all-consuming depression, self-loathing, anxiety, and exhaustion characterize the crack crash (Gawin and Kleber, 1985). Of course, throughout the crash, particularly in earlier stages, the person craves overwhelmingly for more of the drug.

To soften the impending crash many crack users drink alcohol or take minor tranquilizers. Efforts to stay straight contain vivid cocaine dreams. Episodic cravings for the drug are often triggered by seemingly innocuous objects and settings. The person experiences an inability to enjoy the most basic of pleasures due to the exhausted pleasure centers in the limbic system (Cohen, 1985). Despite these powerful physical and psychological experiences, recovery brings the idea that to be off the drug for a brief period means control, which leads to relapse and a quick, precipitous descent to madness once again.

DESIGNER DRUGS

Suppliers are producing more and more drugs which will further test our ability to protect vulnerable young people from very dangerous behaviors. Analogs of drugs have many times the potency of their original substance. These analogs labeled designer drugs are less traceable because of the incredibly small amounts (micrograms rather than milligrams) needed to get high (*Street Pharmacologist*, 1985). Whether crack or a totally new, synthetic compound like fentanyl or MDMA, the trend toward the use of increasingly more powerful, riskier psychoactive compounds causes great concern. As always, the ones at greatest risk from this trend are the most vulnerable, young people.

ATTITUDE TOWARD DRUG USE

Crack should not be a drug of major concern to educators, particularly elementary or middle school educators. That it must be a primary concern represents a dramatic shift in our understanding of the role that prevention strategies must play if young people at risk of becoming substance abusers are to be assisted. Crack is a major league drug, in a class with intravenous heroin use. Only a small proportion of drug users ever advance to such a usage level. Intravenous heroin use is so powerfully reinforcing that it inexorably leads to addiction, dysfunction, and a host of problems like jail, long term treatment, chronic relapse, and death. How do early adolescents become involved in such a nightmare?

By changing the route of administration to smoking, by increasing the potency of the drug, and by packaging it in small, affordable units, drug dealers opened the drug to an entirely new market of freebase cocaine consumers. Teenagers feel comfortable smoking - two of their favorite drugs, nicotine and marijuana, are used this way. The price of crack costs about the same as a bag of grass or a couple of six packs. Given adolescents' traditional feelings of being victimized, of self-doubt, of confusion, of sexual concerns, the drug crack appears tailor-made for them. The drug puts them in charge of themselves and their environment, and for struggling adolescents, there may be no better high.

The public concern about crack recalls a slightly earlier period in our society's chronic failure to come to grips with the necessity of a comprehensive drug prevention policy. In this earlier time, parents sighed with relief when informed that their children were abusing alcohol. "Thank God!" they would say, "It's only alcohol and not that marijuana." I fear that the concern about crack may easily become, "Thank God it's only alcohol and marijuana and not that crack." Because a drug possesses a relatively greater danger than some other drug, the dangers of that other drug are dismissed. As a society we lurch along from one drug crisis to the next, focusing intently on the newest in the line of dangerous drugs.

In fact, attending to one drug misses the point altogether. There is an underlying thread that links all substance abuse together. Substance abuse prevention programs must work along that continuum recognizing that the risk for the individual rises and falls on a range of issues, only one of which is the drug of choice. Individuals who abuse only alcohol because they recognize the riskiness of crack smoking or the health consequences of marijuana or nicotine use, have not, necessarily, minimized their potential for problematic use. Prevention programs and parents must guard against the danger of mistaking the trees for the forest. Prevention strategies must tap into something more basic than the newest drug crisis. They must tap into the person and focus on the personal arena if the risks and benefits of all types of drug use are to be understood.

REFERENCES

Aigner, T.G. & Balster, R.L. (1978). Choice behavior in rhesus monkeys. *Science, 201,* 534-535.

Brenner, J.E. & Kostant, A. (1986). *Cocaine: The Drug That Fell from Grace.* Boston: Ark Publication.

Cohen, S. (1984). Recent developments in the abuse of cocaine. *Bulletin on Narcotics, 36,* 3-14.

_____ (1985) Reinforcement and rapid delivery systems: Understanding adverse consequences of cocaine. In Kozel, N & Adams, E. (Eds.). *Cocaine Use in America: Epidemiologic and Clinical Perspectives.* Rockville, MD: National Institute on Drug Addiction.

Gawin, F. & Kleber, H. (1985). Cocaine use in a treatment population: Patterns and diagnostic distinctions. In Kozel, N. & Adams, E. (Eds.). *Cocaine Use in America: Epidemiologic and Clinical Perspectives.* Rockville, MD: National Institute on Drug Addiction.

Gold, M.S., Washton, A.W. & Dackis, C.A. (1985). Cocaine abuse: Neurochemistry, phenomenology and treatment. In Kozel, N & Adams, E. (Eds.). *Cocaine Use in America: Epidemiologic and Clinical Perspectives.* Rockville, MD: National Institute on Drug Addiction.

Hall, J. (1986). Cocaine smoking ignites America. *Street Pharmacologist, 9,* 1.

Mule, S. (1984). The pharmacodynamics of cocaine abuse. *Psychiatric Annals, 14,* 724-727.

Street Pharmacologist. (1985). Designer Drugs. 8, 5-6.

CHAPTER 4: PREVENTION AND THE PIER PROGRAM

REVIEW

A quick restatement of the concepts so far will help set the stage for a look at prevention. Young people use drugs for a variety of reasons. Whatever their individual reasons, drugs alter chemical processes in all users' brains that change their perceptions and feelings toward themselves and their environment. Both the reasons for use and the effects of the use are best understood in a bio/psycho/social framework.

Prevention strategies need to recognize the interplay of bio/psycho/social factors in initiating use, in continued use, and finally, in addiction. The problem is not peer pressure any more than the solution is to "Just Say No". The situation is more complex than that, so must be the solutions. Finally, the trend toward using more potent substances with smaller windows of safety adds a greater urgency to the work of substance abuse prevention in elementary, middle and secondary schools.

DRUG PREVENTION

What is drug prevention? Not so long ago prevention was considered to be only those activities designed to maintain abstinence or preclude initiation of drug use. Elementary and middle grade students were regarded as non-candidates in regard to drug use, they were too young. When older students announced their candidacy through experimentation with drugs, prevention strategies ceased. Once students experimented with drugs, prevention strategies no longer applied because these activities focused solely on preventing the initiation of use. Moreover, these programs generally provided cognitive strategies that merely emphasized the dangers of any drug use.

This approach failed for a variety of reasons. The living proof rebuttal of classmates or friends, who had tried the very drugs purported to be so dangerous and who not only lived to tell about it but enjoyed the experience, destroyed the credibility of such programs. This approach emphasized cognitive arguments designed to appeal to reason, to influence the decision to use drugs (Hanson, 1980). Young people's decisions to try drugs are usually wrapped in a swirl of needs and expectations that hardly match a conscious determination of choice. The choice grows more from the psyche than the intellect. Prevention programs which appeal to reason alone simply miss the major reasons why youth initiate drug use.

In any prevention effort, abstinence must be the overriding, desired goal. However, narrow definitions of prevention that focus solely on abstinence fail to recognize the important work that must go on after experimentation has begun. Drug abuse prevention must work with individuals at different levels and postures of use. Drug-free and drug-addicted form the two extremes on the expansive continuum of psychoactive substance use. By late adolescence these two extremes don't even describe the majority of teenagers. The vital work for schools, and perhaps the best criterion of the success of their efforts, focuses on how well they help students who fall between the two extremes, the users in danger of becoming abusers.

Substance abuse prevention programming includes those activities designed to:

—support the non-users in their efforts to preclude or delay the initiation of use,

—prevent or delay progression from experimental, infrequent use to the regular use of any substances,

—prevent or delay the expansion of use to other psychoactive substances not presently used by individuals,

—prevent further deterioration among abusers through an appropriate and timely referral.

At each point in users' embrace of a psychoactive drug, they hear the message that this is far enough, that a better way exists, that no need to use is present, that the behavior contains multiple dangers, and people (adults and peers) understand and wish to help. Prevention does not stop when use starts. Its message may change, its format may differ, but it continues to call the user to health. Above all else, prevention continuously approaches students on their using or non-using behavior.

While this may not sound like a lofty goal, prevention has succeeded if students' use does not increase, particularly in the early stages. In drug use, status-quo becomes very heartening. The more schools and teachers can retard if not arrest, and reduce if not remove, the use of present drugs and the expansion to other drugs, the better are youngsters' chances of avoiding or recovering from drug problems. The reason, of course, is time. The younger the users, the more likely the use will eventually become dysfunctional (Kandel, 1978). The more substances used, the greater likelihood of problematic use. The more frequent the use of any drug, and the greater the quantity used, the more likely the use will be troublesome. When prevention strategies delay the movement into more serious usage patterns, young users receive the gift of time, which may change their perspective on the desirability of the behavior in the future.

PIER PROGRAM

The diversity in the goals of a preventive approach requires a program response which is as sophisticated and creative as the young people it seeks to reach. I call this approach a PIER program - Prevention, Intervention, Education, and Referral. A PIER program deals with students at all levels along the use/non-use continuum.

Critical to a successful PIER program is the interdependence of each element on the other. Sound educational efforts on the bio/psycho/social effects of drugs require sound prevention strategies for young persons to develop and build upon. Likewise, effective prevention activities bring to the fore those young people in need of more intensive services like intervention counseling and referral. PIER provides the structure through which a school can develop a program that meets the needs of young people in continual transition concerning their attitudes and behaviors toward drugs.

REFERENCES

Hanson, D.J. (1980). Drug education: Does it work? In Scarpith, E. & Datesman, J. (Eds.). *Drug and Youth Culture.* Beverly Hills, CA: Sage

CHAPTER 5:
EDUCATION—THE
FOUNDATION OF
PIER

DRUG MISEDUCATION

Drug education remains the most misunderstood approach to preventing the use of psychoactive chemicals by young people, in large part because of the unrealistic expectations placed upon it. Some educators equate drug prevention with drug education.

When confronted by a parent on the school's efforts to prevent drug use, a principal may point with pride to the drug curriculum which is taught in every grade in the school. The drug curriculum usually contains accurate information about drugs and their dangers and often includes lessons on values formation so that students have the necessary facts and skills to ward off the dangerous influences that would make them use drugs. The health teacher or the religious studies teacher implements the curriculum in the classroom.

Another school goes a step further and hosts assembly programs in which the students learn the dangers of drugs from people in recovery who relate how awful it was to get high all those years and how great it is to be straight now. When the principal sees little change in the substance abusing patterns of the students, the assertion is made that nothing can be done because of factors beyond the school's control. After all, the school is fulfilling its traditional obligation of teaching children about the dangers of drug use, even using some newer, more innovative approaches in delivering the message. The problem must lie elsewhere.

Across town another school holds little regard for the educational approach to drug prevention. The school's principal examined articles which proved that teaching students about drugs was worse than ineffective, it was downright dangerous and raised their curiosity which led to increased not decreased use. Drug education was counter-productive (Polich, et al., 1984). Besides, educating students about the dangers of drugs amounted to little more than scare tactics, which just don't work with today's student. Often the stories don't match young people's experiences which then erode teachers' credibility.

How can a method serve as the centerpiece for one school's approach and be totally rejected by another school as damaging and dangerous? The answer resides in expectations. The first school sees drug use as a consequence of misinformed behavior which is open to influence by a rational approach. The second school builds upon the rational approach by introducing an emotional, scare approach, but denies the influence that the school can have on outside factors. The third school, observing some of the limitations in the educational approach and the risks in such a strategy, surrenders, thus denying students access to the pure, unadulterated truth.

What can information do to affect youngsters' behaviors concerning their use or non-use of drugs and alcohol? A school can do a great deal when it has clear and realistic goals for its drug education program.

GOALS OF DRUG EDUCATION

Drug education (the E in the PIER program) is not a drug prevention program. When a school equates the two, it gets neither useful education nor effective prevention. Education is only one of several components in a drug prevention program. The educational component provides information so that informed choices can be made. Since substance abuse involves emotional responses, decisions to use or to expand use are rarely rational. Information about the drug and its dangers does not, in and of itself, lead to abstinence. When a school relies too heavily on a cognitive approach to prevent drug abuse, it has chosen a vehicle ill-equipped to affect the students' behavior.

Drug education establishes an atmosphere of awareness in a school, drug use is discussed openly and seriously in such an institution. Drug education works continuously against the dynamic of denial in an individual, a student body, a school faculty, administration, parents and, finally, the community or parish at large.

A most tragic irony of the disease of chemical dependency in individuals is that the sicker addicts become, the more difficulty they have in recognizing the cause of their problem. The more that the drug comes to dominate their lives, the more they come to rely on the drug as the only reality, the only thing that makes sense. Such people deny the source of their troubles, even as they embrace drugs wholeheartedly. No other disease has quite that pathetic dynamic of denial leading to increased reliance on what is making one ill in the first place.

The dynamic of denial extends to systems. Families often choose to deny the existence of a problem, "She's young, she'll grow out of it." "He's under a lot of stress." Some schools follow the same pattern. Principals and teachers have spoken to me about the awful consequences of the youthful drug problem and ended by saying, "But thank God, not here!" How one school is spared the problem of drug abuse when all around it other schools have serious troubles is never explained. Schools may deny the problem as a means of avoiding the need for action. If even one student in a school experiments with drugs, the school has a drug problem. Such a school needs a comprehensive program because a life is in danger. Catholic educators respect all life.

An active, publicly endorsed program of drug education works against the denial. In fact it encourages acknowledgement of the problem which sets the stage for meaningful change. Drug education is the backdrop or context within which the real work of drug prevention, intervention, and referral takes place. Education creates the atmosphere which recognizes youngsters' genuine struggle to confront the reality of their drug use option. Public acknowledgement also permits the young users to reach out for help. Education creates the foundation upon which drug prevention efforts can rest.

DRUG EDUCATION IN A CATHOLIC SCHOOL

Drug education can be diverse and creative in its approach. I find somewhat puzzling the fact that few Catholic schools ground their drug education and prevention efforts in the Christian principles which give the school its purpose and meaning. Somehow teaching students about drugs, their effects, and their consequences is viewed as separate or different from the mission of the school. The prevention activities do not express the unique circumstances of Christians and their role in this world. The significance of the individual to Jesus and His healing power in the face of whatever difficulties are not intellectual artifacts found in the school's mission statement but living, dynamic realities that define and express the Christian's experience. To discuss the facts of contemporary substance abuse independent of the Gospel message fractures the fundamental mission of the Catholic school and does a disservice to the students who struggle to make sense of a world in which feeling and looking good takes precedence over doing or being good.

The similarities between choices about psychoactive drug use and choices about spiritual matters are not merely superficial. Drugs change people's feelings (affective response) about themselves and their environment. Christian belief also promotes a new reality, that the world and the individual are different, not because of the actions of psychoactive chemicals but from a transformation of the individual based on and in Jesus. This new reality, the Christian reality, should be as intoxicating as the modern-day pharmacopeia, however it is rarely experienced as such, or even sought to be experienced as such. The good news is often experienced by youngsters as old news.

If substance abuse is a chemical transformation that is ultimately self-destructive, religious schools should seize the opportunity to weave into the fabric of their prevention programs the intoxicating experience of spiritual transformation which is ultimately self-redeeming. Beginning with the drug education component, drug prevention efforts must be grounded in and express the living reality of Jesus as the context and at times the content of drug prevention in a Catholic school.

PRESENTING THE FACTS

Drug education activities should avoid stretching the facts. When teachers present the bio/psycho/social facts to students with appropriate emphasis on the extraordinary challenges the students face, the facts speak for themselves. To try to do more with the facts may risk the teachers' credibility. The battleground in terms of youngsters' eventual behavior with drugs should never be over the truths associated with drugs. Teachers who try to get more from the facts by portraying use and its consequences in the most extreme instances are ignored or ridiculed. Students know others who get high, such youth may be sitting next to them in class or at the dinner table. To predict the most dire consequences for drug consumers when their immediate experience contradicts this portrayal does more harm than good.

While information needs to be accurate so that youth can relate the facts to their experiences, educators should not believe that their students know a great deal about drugs. An enduring myth to survive the initial explosion of drug use by young people in the 1960's states that youngsters know more about drugs than adults. A corollary states that users know more about drugs than anybody. Neither is particularly truthful. Woeful levels of ignorance exist among young people, particularly users, about the effects of psychoactive drugs on their bodies. Drug users, particularly polydrug users, are often even unsure what they may have taken on any given occasion, particularly those drugs that follow the initial use of some drugs. Young students do not necessarily know the simple, basic facts about their drug of choice and what the use of it means to them.

Middle grade students have almost no idea of how psychoactive drugs mimic, facilitate, or impair the normal operation of the brain. What they do know about drugs is experiential, i.e., how they feel when they use, and how they feel because they use. When drug education becomes construed by drug using adolescents as challenging their knowledge, their defenses go up. They will aggressively defend their knowledge because of the threat that an accurate depiction of the facts presents to their sense of self and their identity as drug users. Adults who misread the dynamic and challenge youngsters' experience with the facts will not be heeded, no matter how dangerous the circumstances may appear to the older, wiser guardians.

Whether speaking to a group of inmates in a state correctional institution or to an assembly of students, I stake out my territory very early and refuse to surrender it no matter what the challenge. "I am an expert," I tell them, "on drugs: what drugs do, how drugs do it, and why people use drugs. I am not an expert on you, or your reactions to the drugs that you may have used." I defer to their judgment in the presentations when they tell me how they or a "friend" reacted to a particular drug. I do not defer to their judgment, however, on how or what a drug does to the body or the psyche. Once we get clear who is the expert on what, we now can hear what the other says. We both benefit from the exchange. People do not know about drugs and alcohol in the most important ways. Drug education expands their awareness, it does not deny their experience with this risky and seductive practice.

Drug education activities include the traditional curriculum, assemblies, forums, parents' nights, awareness days, audio-visual presentations, and any medium which disseminates and explores relevant information on the use of psychoactive drugs. To this list should be added a comprehensive, written policy on drug use which expresses a philosophy of chemical dependency. Liturgical and paraliturgical services should be used to enliven the participants to their new reality of being Christians and how the life of Jesus models a healthy and strong self-concept.

The overall purpose of drug education seeks not only to inform but also to develop an atmosphere of awareness or context for more intensive drug prevention and intervention efforts. The willingness of the school to acknowledge the challenge that psychoactive drugs present to the individual and to the community of faith is the first step in addressing it and eventually, preventing it. Drug education begins that process.

REFERENCES

Polich, J.M., Ellickson, P.L., Reuter, P. & Kahan, J. P. (1984). *Strategies for Controlling Adolescent Drug Use.* Santa Monica: The Rand Corporation.

CHAPTER 6: PREVENTION - WORKING WITH STUDENTS

INTRODUCTION

The heart of a school's response to the problem of youthful substance abuse is in its prevention component (the P in the PIER approach). Prevention programming makes the difference between success and disaster for students. No matter how effectively a school educates students for the modern world, if it does not provide them with the decision-making skills needed to determine the personal use of psychoactive chemicals, it has failed in its responsibility to the students. The prevalence of use and the availability of every type of drug in every community makes the reality of choosing to use or not, a direct, unavoidable issue for youngsters. The social dimension of use and the public nature of the experience leaves little room for equivocation. A school that refuses to see the essential aspects of this dilemma for its students and to help them explore this reality does not understand the youth culture in America. The process of making clear the choice and of making conscious what is now left too often to the unconscious forms the drug prevention component.

PREVENTION

Prevention programming affords students the opportunity to examine their world in light of the question of personal use of psychoactive chemicals. Furthermore, through the process of examination, teenagers develop the skills to make responsible decisions about the use of these chemicals. The prevention component of a school's substance abuse prevention program ensures that so basic an issue as drug use does not resolve itself by chance or default. A myriad of forums and experiences frames and reframes the issue, "What does this behavior mean for me?"

Public health practitioners divide prevention into three levels with each level reflecting a higher degree of risk of contracting a disease. Primary prevention services seek to eliminate the occurrence of the problem in the general population, without regard for any special set of factors that places an individual at risk of initiating the behavior. Secondary prevention services target people with some evidence of being at higher risk than the general population (for example, some initial experience with drugs or having some identifiable risk factor such as children of alcoholic parents). Tertiary prevention services, also known as early intervention, attend to individuals with some evidence of the disease, for example, a person with a substance abuse problem who is not as yet dysfunctional.

The primary, secondary, and tertiary descriptions of prevention services enable the development and implementation of strategies specifically targeted to certain populations at greater risk. However, educators should recall that all students need to be educated on all aspects of psychoactive substances no matter where they are on the prevention continuum.

Prevention and education differ in their methods and their purposes. The methods and activities of each component are appropriate for young people, regardless of their present drug using status. Education informs and influences; prevention personalizes and concertizes the issue.

The school-based prevention program's first goal seeks to support students in their decision not to use drugs. A school may be tempted to minimize its program for non-using adolescents based on the belief that, "These students would never use drugs." Substance abuse is an equal opportunity destroyer. If a particular student was somehow exempt from all the pressures of adolescence, no more could be said of that person than, "This child has never used drugs." People and circumstances change, never more so than in the pre-adolescent and adolescent years.

Guiding young people through the turbulence and the seductive allure of immediate relief through drug use does not allow for exemptions based on current performance.

Fortunately, the non-use of drugs is a condition that reinforces itself over time. Each new circumstance does not induce a crisis of choice for those young persons. Unfortunately, the use of drugs is also a condition that reinforces itself over time. Young people can move from non-use to regular abuse in the course of a summer. The prevention program continues to support non-users in their continued non-use. A prevention component that triages its targets and excludes the non-user places many more students at risk.

On the other hand, a school's prevention effort which focuses exclusively on the non-user and views this work as the only worthwhile, realistic goal of a school-based service misses the single most significant group amenable to prevention programming strategies, the early or experimental user. A prevention program can arrest, reduce and even eliminate periodic use by some adolescents. Prevention strategies challenge the experimental or regular users of gateway drugs like alcohol and marijuana to examine their use as it relates to their sense of self, their current circumstances, and their future. The questions surrounding teenage drug use remain as valid for the episodic user as for the non-user. The programming objective for both seeks to make conscious, controlled and, therefore, intended, what to date may be an unconscious and unexamined behavior.

In helping users to examine their behavior, the outcome is almost always positive, even when there is no immediate reduction in current use. Owning their behaviors requires teenagers to evaluate them before moving forward into more frequent use and use of more potent drugs. Helping experimental users to consider and control their use creates the first step in stopping the use. Controlled or arrested use is a step in a process that most individuals eventually take of their own accord. For those youths unable to take that step on their own, programming helps them examine their behavior and may move them in the desired direction.

Prevention programming helps in two other areas. It delays or precludes the expansion of use to other psychoactive substances, and it can identify adolescents already in serious difficulty with drugs who need more intensive services.

Research has identified additional difficulties for individuals trying to recover from polydrug abuse. Kandel (1978) and her associates found a clear distinction in the psychological functioning of youth who used marijuana and alcohol and adolescents who used another drug in addition to grass and alcohol. No such dichotomy exists between non-users and the users of marijuana and alcohol.

The final goal, identifying children in need of more intensive services, flows from the above components of an effective prevention program. When a safe forum exists to consider the drug question, students in trouble ask for help. If a school has developed a meaningful prevention effort, it engenders the trust of those who need it most.

ELEMENTS OF EFFECTIVE PREVENTION PROGRAMS

Many prevention strategies have common elements which are affective or behavioral in design not didactic or informational. Prevention activities foster a sense of personal mastery through self-exploration and skill-acquisition. Throughout the prevention component are the threads of self-exploration, self-discovery, and self-acceptance.

Drug prevention activities have the distinctive characteristic of linking consciously the needs, hopes, and self-expressions of teens to the issue of drug use. The prevention activity seeks to have the participants realize the relative dangers and risks of drug abuse for themselves and their friends. Such a realization springs not from a packaged message given to individuals, but arises through the process of self-examination.

Theme-centered and time-limited prevention activities have a sense of organization and purpose. A group comes together for a specific purpose, which may or may not relate directly to substance abuse issues, conducts the activity and in the process learns about themselves, each other and the question of substance abuse. The learning process can at times be hidden and indistinguishable from more apparent objectives. However, at some point in the life of the group, each member examines the issues. The group leader focuses the group on the issue of substance abuse and the individual members' responses to it.

The group may disband or incorporate new members after completing a specific purpose. Substance abuse prevention occurs in a number of forums, some of which are created expressly for the purpose of preventing drug abuse by students and their families while others foster prevention in an indirect manner.

Prevention activities have a present orientation, meeting some present needs of the students. Even when the activity is future oriented, the need to explore the future should be an immediate one and shared by the group members. The success of the activity depends upon the close relationship of the activity to the needs of the individuals. The real question posed in prevention activities focuses on the personal relevance of drug use considerations to individuals. Consequently, the activity must touch a felt need or desire in the present. The activity should be grounded in the general psychosocial developmental needs of the participants and it should have an immediate, practical and stimulating purpose.

Peer Programming

The most effective set of prevention activities in my experience employs a peer programming approach. Whatever the actual content, peer programming places the responsibility for helping someone in a matter of personal importance squarely on the shoulders of the students themselves. Peer programming, a powerful concept, particularly among those students most susceptible to the peer dynamic (middle school and early high school years), takes advantage of the developmental needs of pre-teens and teens for affiliation and group validation and channels those needs into a creative process for preventing substance abuse.

A peer approach can serve as the foundation for a prevention program for all grade levels. Older students working with younger students in thematic groups in drug education and in social services like tutoring serve the dual purpose of involving older youth in a worthwhile project (having them critically examine their own using behavior as part of their training), while creatively meeting an educational need at the primary level.

The real attractiveness of a peer approach is its flexibility and adaptability. For example, the Archdiocese of

New York Drug Abuse Prevention Program (ADAPP) recognized the serious difficulty many freshmen students encountered in leaving the neighborhood elementary school for a larger, geographically distant high school. With the added stress of forming new peer relationships in this new environment, the potential for initial or increased drug and alcohol use was great. ADAPP set up transition groups for students deemed to be at high risk and held sessions through the summer and into the school year until new friendships were created. It used a peer-dominated, mutual-aid approach to the problems of adapting to a new environment and its strong potential for substance abuse.

In any peer approach that utilizes young people in a helping mode, the quality of the training and the supervision of the work determine the eventual success of the program. The importance of training and supervision cannot be overstated in maintaining a peer counseling program. Peer counselors need a great deal of help in learning how to set boundaries; in giving and receiving feedback; in reaching for feelings; in active listening skills like empathy, reflection, and clarification; in exploring alternatives and seeking closure; in matters of confidentiality; and, most especially, in the referral process for those students in need of professional help. Peer counselors must explore their own attitudes and how to use their own unique attributes and styles in the helping process.

A school needs both an active training program for their peer counselors and an effective program of supervision of the counselors' work. Peer counselors need support if they are to be effective. Young people left on their own to work with peers or younger students on personal issues will quickly become overwhelmed and frustrated. Peer counselors need the validation from each other and adults who understand the strengths and limitations in this approach. They also need to feel like they are getting something from their work, which may mean social and recreational as well as psychological rewards. Well-trained, well-supervised, enthusiastic peer counselors offer a tremendous resource to a school in its efforts to engage the entire school community in the mission of prevention.

The counselors benefit most from the peer program because they learn more about themselves and receive more from each other than they can realistically give to others. Everyone who participates in the program, as a group member, a peer leader, a faculty adviser, or a trainer derives some personal benefit from an effective program. The school itself derives a great benefit because of the attention paid to the question of what can be done to help students on a variety of issues, including drug use. Additional benefits of peer programming include fresh programming ideas and a quick response to unanticipated, newly developing issues among students.

Peer programming has extended well beyond its initial emphasis on counseling to a more general definition of service to a group of contemporaries or (in some cases) younger students. Many secondary schools and colleges now train their varsity athletes, to talk with elementary school children on drug-related matters. Using a curriculum of four or five sessions, the athletes talk with the younger students about drugs, peer pressure, and how to feel good about themselves through activities like sports. Similar peer approaches can be used with junior high and high school groups with more advanced skills and in areas of interest, e.g., creative writing, journalism, theatre arts, story-telling, music, rap and break dancing. Whatever the individuals' skills and interests, the prevention program puts them to work, first to examine their own issues vis a vis drug use, and then to use the interest in the activity to help others. The programming potential is as vast as are the individuals' interests.

Counter-normative Strategies

Many secondary schools have also added a series of counter-normative programming strategies that not only involve young people in prevention activities but challenge the current teenage norms about drug and alcohol use. Students Against Driving Drunk (SADD) is an excellent example of counter-normative programming. Such groups are a welcomed addition to drug prevention efforts because they participate in forums not readily available to adults: the public opinion arenas of teenagedom. SADD members in their own way develop the prevention goal of making conscious and intended the choice of using drugs and alcohol. Other programs like "Dial-A-Ride" (provides help or a ride home if one has been using a psychoactive chemical), or "Safe Homes" (a guarantee by parents to other parents of supervision and a drug-free environment for adolescents visiting their homes) and other school and community-based projects such as drug-free dance clubs and cafes are also effective. They work on a number of levels to dispel the prevailing notions that the use of chemicals by youth goes unnoticed by adults; that parents remain powerless to do anything about the problem except to worry; that drug or alcohol use by youngsters is a private affair not open to scrutiny; and that drugs can be indulged in indiscriminately.

The more the school and community acknowledge the public nature of the problem through public-oriented, ongoing programming, the more difficult it is for youngsters to ignore their own personal use and its implications. Home-school associations can play a vital role in this type of counter-normative, public, ongoing programming.

Extra-curricular Activites

Extra-curricular activities and programs also offer natural environments in which drug prevention themes emerge. Extra-curricular events need not be turned into a drug prevention seminar, however rich opportunities exist in these settings for a brief, intimate look at the issue if the advisor catches the signals. The perspective in these discussions is unique and personal; it is grounded in the activity itself and people's reasons for being there. Why learn music, dance, soccer, chess, computers, or the thousands of other activities which all enjoy and in some instances love passionately?

The selection of an activity announces a personal statement, perhaps muted and indistinguishable at times, but nevertheless a statement by the people choosing that activity. That connection usually unexamined by students but often scrutinized by adults provides hints as to why they enjoy a particular activity so much. Participation in activities and clubs and recognition of their meaning to people serve as behavioral counterpoints to feeling good about themselves and handling negative feelings through drug use.

Within these activities, opportunities arise to ask the students or small groups of students why they participate and what they derive from these activities. While answers like, "It's fun" or "I don't know, I just like it" are to be expected, with some gentle questioning, students will make the connection between what they do, who they are, and how this may apply to other issues. Students begin to view the activity as a resource, a way of feeling good that they can count on when they don't feel so good. These moments afford teachers wonderful opportunities to step outside their traditional teaching posture to share why they too are there and what they derive from the conduct of this activity. Extra-curricular activities provide for some methods of personal coping, of caring, and of valuing the self. They are some of the ways people have learned to deal with and take pleasure in living.

Extra-curricular work because it reflects people's personal choices and activities provides a rather intimate portrait of how they deal with life. Students make similar choices when they select extra-curricular activities. The connections among self, affective expression, and emotional resources can be discovered in the regular course of an extra-curricular activity. Moreover, such choices enlarge the chasm that exists between this self-enhancing approach to life and the self-negating approach of psychoactive chemical use. Adolescents learn to realize that ways exist to feel good about themselves which are easily accessible. Extra-curricular advisors with a passion for their activities can help their charges realize this.

Meditation

An area of prevention work that remains oddly underdeveloped in most schools falls into a category which is best described as alternate consciousness. Although this category could include any kind of activity that offers the possibility of a euphoric experience like sports or music, I prefer to categorize these traditional activities as extra-curricular.

Underdeveloped in my estimation in most schools but less understandably so in Catholic schools are activities geared toward developing alternative highs through alternate consciousness. Catholicism has a rich tradition of mysticism and prayer through meditation. Yet somehow the strengths of meditation, placing oneself in the presence of God and examining one's relationship to self, others and the divinity, are not aggressively developed or encouraged.

Meditation and contemplation are preventive strategies that have a renewed power for this world. People don't know how to be with themselves, much less with their God (sometimes I wonder if one is the pre-requisite of the other). For many, the pace of life, the level of noise, the emphasis on materialism and acquisition of goods have caused a profound depersonalization from self, each other, and, ultimately, from God. Being still in this frenetic society, seeking spiritual realities, and transcending the immediate are powerful means not only of drug prevention but of genuine self-fulfillment. The absence of a greater emphasis on meditation and its regular practice in life is a failing in today's society. Catholicism has something most profound to offer young people as an alternative to a drug-induced euphoria and its teachers should be more active in fostering it.

All forms of meditation can exercise a preventive function in terms of drug abuse. Transcendental meditation, deep breathing and imaging programs, self-hypnosis, and eastern meditations can have a salutary effect on the soul and the psyche. Alcoholics Anonymous, the most successful treatment for long term recovery from chemical dependency, understood the spiritual roots of a problem with alcohol. The first two steps in the twelve step recovery process call for the individuals to admit powerlessness in the face of alcohol and to acknowledge a power greater than themselves to call upon in seeking sobriety. Carl Jung once defined every problem over the age of 25 as having a spiritual component. Jung interpreted alcoholism as a poorly organized, destructive attempt in the search for wholeness, which in religious thought reflected the person's longing for God (Kinney and Leaton, 1987). If the cure for chemical dependency is in part spiritual, then surely its prevention is partly spiritual. Catholic schools should be looking for ways to incorporate their tradition of meditation and alternative consciousness into their drug prevention component.

Special Events

A school year has a life and a rhythm of its own. Within the general school calendar certain grades have events that serve as markers of students' status in the school. The events often reflect the psycho-social level of the students as well. Both the general school calendar and the special events within the school year offer unique opportunities for students to explore their attitudes toward drugs and peer pressure. For example, the Teen Club which is the preserve of eighth graders provides an opportunity for young people to look at themselves and their peers critically as they set the rules of behavior for attending the club. Even if no one has ever come intoxicated or high to the Teen Club, an honest discussion about the possibility and the consequences forces a serious look at the behavior, particularly if the moderators commit themselves to following those procedures.

Even in younger grades there are special opportunities to look at substance abuse. Discussions of celebrations like Christmas and what it means to celebrate can reveal interesting (and at times horrifying) accounts on the role of alcohol (and other drugs) in the celebration. The class bus trip can lead to a discussion of safety considerations on the road and the danger of alcohol use when driving. Participation in the perennial substance abuse prevention month with in-class skits, posters, or writing exercises on prevention themes provides a positive vehicle to start students and teachers thinking. Substance abuse is an everyday phenomenon in America which is no longer on the periphery of most people's experience. Substance abuse prevention, therefore, should not be treated as a peripheral activity in school, relegated to certain prescribed activities by certain professionals.

The limited opportunities to bring a prevention theme into some aspect of teaching should not constrain any more than the limitations of talking about other real life issues in school. Children benefit when the approach continually pulls the question into the open. When teachers seize the opportunities to develop prevention themes within their classes, based on some aspect of the school year or some matter of personal relevance to the children, the importance of the issue reverberates throughout the school.

COMPONENTS OF A SUCCESSFUL PROGRAM

The prevention component of a comprehensive PIER substance abuse prevention program has room for everyone, and works best when the faculty genuinely supports the efforts. Even with that, there are keys to successful prevention programming which increase the likelihood of success in affecting young people's behavior.

1. Programming should be personal, present-oriented, and relevant to the students' interests and needs.

Children judge the effectiveness of substance abuse prevention programs. Adults' needs are quite secondary in what is essentially a program to influence the personal decisions of students. Those decisions will be reaffirmed or modified behaviorally throughout their years in school and well beyond. To influence the process, the programming must meet their needs and communicate in their language. Teachers cannot keep youngsters from experimenting with drugs any more than parents can keep their children from growing up.

Prevention of drug use is not like a polio vaccine, guaranteed to inoculate the recipient against the disease. In order to help, teachers must be willing to forego the assumption that "Teacher knows best," not because it isn't true but because it doesn't matter. What does matter is children's experiences of themselves, of friends and family. The suspension of the solution in order to allow for the legitimate struggle that most teenagers face concerning their options paves the way in the long run for the advice or support to be accepted when finally offered.

2. Students should be involved in the program's design.

The peer dynamic makes the ownership of the prevention program a serious issue. If the peer leaders or the participants in the prevention activities are construed by their peers to be mini-adults espousing the rhetoric and the agenda of the adult world, the program, no matter how creative, will have minimal impact. The student body must own the program. The activities, events, discussions, groups, etc. must be student endorsed and responsive to student needs. The best way to assure this is to bring the students into the planning process as much as possible. Again, the more students struggle to help other students, the more they all benefit and the stronger the program.

3. Programming should be periodically reviewed and renewed.

Nothing is more boring than yesterday's news. In prevention programming, failure to regenerate the program with new ideas and activities along with new blood to develop those ideas will spell defeat in the long term. Peer programming in particular suffers when overexposed and underrenewed. Programming concepts get tired when used for too long; the students sense the complacency and lose interest as well. The school must be willing to look at its prevention strategies critically and to develop other responses. The philosophy doesn't change, only its expression.

4. An active, responsive in-service component is important to develop teacher skill and to generate faculty enthusiasm for the effort.

Creativity is at a premium during a school year when teacher responsibilities outstrip teacher time and energy. A suggestion to be creative doesn't help much when questions of method and outcome get raised. The development and implementation of a comprehensive prevention program require specialized skills and the time to accomplish the goal. That is not the teachers' responsibility. Within the development of the prevention program there still must be a structure to assist teachers in exploring prevention themes in their classrooms.

Everyone must be involved in drug prevention work. The administration, the faculty, the student service personnel, the extra-curricular advisors, and the students themselves and their parents, can contribute to the development and maintenance of a dynamic, diverse, responsive prevention program. The entire school's participation in some detail of a prevention effort will give the program a vitality and an ownership that promises success. Everyone can contribute something to the prevention effort and should be encouraged to do so.

REFERENCES

Kandel, D. (Ed.). (1978) *Longitudinal Research on Drug Use: Empirical Findings and Methodological Issues.* Washington, DC: Hemisphere-Wiley.

Kinney, J. & Leaton, G. (1987). *Loosening the Grip* (3rd ed.). St. Louis: Times Mirror/Mosby College Publishing.

CHAPTER 7:
INTERVENTION AND
REFERRAL-TIMELY HELP

RELATIONSHIP TO EDUCATION
AND PREVENTION

The best efforts of drug education and prevention will not erase the need for intervention counseling in a PIER program. The more responsive these activities become to student issues, the more apparent will the need for intervention counseling appear. Some children will experiment with psychoactive chemicals and some will develop serious problems as a result of these trials. The intervention counseling and referral components (the "I" and the "R" in PIER) respond to those troubled children.

While it may seem paradoxical that the more effective a school becomes in preventing substance abuse, the more it may appear to have a serious problem of substance abuse among its students, the reality is quite a different matter. The dynamic of denial which keeps individuals from seeing their problem with psychoactive chemicals operates at a systemic level as well. In the denial of the existence of a drug problem, the school and the substance abusers form an unspoken conspiracy which allows each to operate under a delusion of control. The school institutes a weak, mediocre prevention program consisting mainly of information and exhortations to stay away from drugs. The fact that the prevention program does not uncover any students or families with substance abuse problems only confirms the effectiveness of the approach. The school never personalizes the drug question for students. The program never establishes an environment in which drugs can be talked about honestly.

In the meantime, drug using students remain unchallenged. Their own denial of any problem complements the school's denial. Both feel in control of a behavior which may be growing out of control. The school's unwillingness to confront the issue of drugs in their students' lives reinforces the destructive process operating at the individual level. The management by denial approach results in a loss for students who quickly learn that school is not a place to talk about these things or to get help in resolving them.

If the school has no need for intervention counseling or for an active referral program, the education and prevention components are in all likelihood ineffective. When prevention activities are meaningful to students they manifest concern for themselves, a sibling, a friend, a parent, anyone who is affected by this disease. The intention of the activities is to generate that concern so that the reality of the choice and its consequences are made present. Prevention programming that does not personalize the issue, that plays it safe and never challenges, can not affect attitudes and behavior. Prevention/education is supposed to "cause" problems for a school, in the sense of uncovering what was previously unacknowledged. A good indication that a school's prevention program is preventing future problems (or at least their possibility) lies in the number and kind of problems being discovered in the present.

Schools need an intervention/referral capacity to complement the work of the prevention and education components. Drug prevention programs may become inundated by the counseling and treatment needs of students and their families. Prevention-oriented teachers and peer leaders may become frustrated at their inability to meet the growing demands on their time and their emotional resources. They are not equipped to handle the clinical needs of troubled students. The absence of an intervention counseling resource increases their own workload. The prevention effort collapses under the weight of the demand for specialized services which were unforeseen in the initial development of prevention services.

INTERVENTION

Many students will need professional help in working through their personal and family problems related to substance abuse. Schools can provide the help directly through special counseling programs or indirectly through a well-established and clearly defined school/community referral system. The intervention component requires a planned response involving specialized personnel, community counseling agencies, and a detailed protocol on how each works with the other.

Intervention counseling may reach the fewest number of students directly, but its influence extends well beyond its reach. Intervention counseling challenges users to confront a behavior that may have become as comfortable as their favorite pair of jeans. The process, when done correctly, can freeze, reduce, or eliminate students' current patterns of use. Moreover, the struggle to reject the behavior also plays a role in a school-based prevention program. Recovering youth provide eloquent testimony not only to the dangers of drug abuse but to the promise of change. Regardless of the problem, adolescents who see other teenagers in a recovery process receive a two-fold message: 1) that problems are better shared than hidden, 2) and that the place to get help is school. For students with drug problems or with drug problems at home, observing a schoolmate receiving help provides powerful motivation.

The education, cognitive, component of PIER emphasizes accurate drug information and understanding processes such as decision-making and peer pressure. The prevention component, essentially affective in design, emphasizes personal feelings and the skill to reject the pressures to use drugs. Intervention counseling with its behavioral design emphasizes students' self-defeating behaviors, the consequences of their behavior, and adaptive ways of behaving. The accent focuses on behavioral changes, on acquiring new ways to handle old problems and current feelings.

Sally Shields, the Executive Director of the Archdiocese of New York Drug and Alcohol Prevention Program (ADAPP), has described ADAPP's successful intervention work with substance abusing secondary school students.

She has applied the principles of the interactive group work model of William Schwartz (1961, 1971) to a school-based intervention service. Through peer-oriented, interactive group sessions, ADAPP's counselors enable the students and the school to "recognize their stake in each other" and to "reach out to the other in more effective ways" (Shields, 1986). ADAPP's intervention focus crystallizes a fundamental value for the school: substance abuse affects more than the individual and solutions to this problem must involve the school as a nurturing system for young people.

In modern America young people may initiate drug use for a variety of reasons, some of which are not amenable to a prevention solution. Whatever the motivation, drug use by young people at some point in their adolescent years is a cause for concern for themselves and others. When teenagers continue to use and move on to more frequent use of more diverse substances, alarms should go off loudly and clearly. Intervention counseling targets these young people before their drug use becomes so ingrained as to create another whole set of drug-related problems with the law, the family and the school. Counseling helps students to sort through their behaviors and feelings with supportive and direct approaches in order to seek the unspoken truth. Intervention counseling includes: identification and expression of the affective, relating affective to behavior, especially the drug behavior, and exploring other ways of meeting personal needs.

Like prevention, intervention counseling uses the group setting and the peer dynamic to work with students. Through a here and now orientation that does not allow the group to dwell on matters beyond their control or behaviors outside the group's observation, the students talk about themselves and their experiences in a system of mutual support which breaks down their isolation, their fear of exposure, and their mistrust. Getting high is examined in an individual and group context.

CHARACTERISTICS OF STUDENTS USING DRUGS

What is different about youth who develop problems with chemicals? The literature contains studies which assert and reject a variety of personality attributes found more prevalent in one population than the other. In reality we don't know if any exist.

For some youngsters, the drug experience works. Through the pharmacological effects of the drug or through the acquired sense of belonging and identification with a drug using peer group, the drug experience comforts some teens like nothing else has. Youth in recovery often report that they never felt quite right or connected in their peer group before using drugs. They would go to great lengths to mask their discomfort and vulnerability. When they were high those feelings of separation dissolved. Drug use became the unifying theme and the shared, common experience in the group's life which pushed away the doubts and insecurities. Intervention counseling efforts break through the isolation and fear so characteristic of drug using youngsters.

In my work with young people I have noticed some common deficits among youths in trouble with drugs. They are hardly unique to drug using students and many teachers will have seen the same obstacles in their work with troubled students. However, these characteristics bear mentioning as areas for special attention.

1. Inability to view themselves in development - Some drug using children have not fully developed what psychologists call an observing ego, the ability to see themselves, their circumstances, and the consequences of a certain behavior in terms of personal considerations and future goals. These adolescents show a marked inability to delay, to pause and to consider before acting. Such impulsiveness makes them unable to say "No" to any of the myriad of opportunities to drink or to do drugs. While high their impulsive actions may lead to physical aggression, speeding while driving, or playing chicken while drunk or other forms of self-destructive behaviors.

2. Inability to tolerate frustration and anxiety - The substance abuse literature has long described substance abusers as having a marked inability to persevere in the face of difficult tasks or to tolerate the heightened levels of frustration and anxiety attendant to those tasks. Drug using

71

teens in a society dominated by the electronic media often feel quite frustrated and blocked by an adult world that simultaneously baffles and challenges. The adult world presents consistent though at times subtle messages that negative mood states are not tolerated, that something is wrong in feeling bad, or that negative feelings are easily dealt with.

While many teens have difficulty understanding or realizing negative mood states, e.g., anxiety, depression and anger, drug using teens often have difficulty even getting in touch with their feelings. Such youngsters seek the quick resolution mind set that is part of the contextual backdrop of modern America, "If you don't feel good, change the feeling." Lacking problem-solving skills they opt for the next best thing, mood change through chemicals.

3. Inability to value themselves - Much of the work with drug using adolescents centers on their feelings about themselves. The sense of worthlessness which characterizes so many of these young people has led me to reconsider Jesus's notable injunction to "Love your neighbor as yourself" and examine its application to these adolescents. Drug abusing youngsters often treat others exactly the way they feel about themselves, unloved and worthless. Underneath this typical veneer of self-importance, they see little worthy of even their own attention. Some youth don't love themselves, and their actions demonstrate their indifference and disregard. Behaviors that shout, "I don't care!" also whisper, "I'm not worth caring about." Getting high and staying high make perfect sense in so bleak a world. Group counseling, intensive group experiences like retreats, and teachers that see through the behavior (even while not accepting it) communicate what is the prerequisite realization for stopping and staying off drugs, "You are indeed cared for and worth caring about." For young persons who repel people with hostility and numb their own psyche with drugs this realization can be redemptive.

4. Inability to develop interests and to derive pleasure from them - Drug abuse can very quickly become an exclusionary interest. Nothing quite matches the short-lived euphoria that comes from anticipating, getting and being high. Hobbies, interests, and people pale in comparison to the rush and comfort of a drug-induced euphoria. Unfortunately some students experience their first truly captivating experience when they get high. For other students, formerly pleasurable habits lose their lustre. In either case, drug users derive less and less enjoyment from common pleasures and personal hobbies. Prevention programming challenges the boredom which many adolescents experience as crushing and blanketing. Getting young people excited and involved decreases the attractiveness and the allure of drug and alcohol use.

Children Of Alcoholics - A Special Problem

Approximately 14,000,000 people in this country are alcoholics or regarded as problem drinkers. Charles Deutsch (1982), a noted author on the problems of children of alcoholics, gave a most apt definition of a problem drinker as an "alcoholic who you care about." Alcohol abuse exercises a pre-eminently destructive role in all aspects of life. Nowhere are the effects of alcohol more poignant than in the troubled lives of the children of alcoholic parents. Unfortunately, children in alcoholic families often work especially hard to hide from those who can help their pain and their parents' condition out of a sense of guilt, of responsibility or of despair.

Children in alcoholic families often express the family's pain as well as its hopes in stereotypical ways. Well-behaved, overachieving, hero children carry the alcoholic family's failed aspirations along with the family secret of parental drinking and discord (Black, 1979). Rebellious, acting-out children express the pain and anger in the family by attempting to deflect attention from the real cause of the problems in the family, the alcoholic parent. Other children take on roles to survive in the inconsistent, troubled, and often frightening world of a family living with an active alcoholic (Wegscheider, 1979). The studies of Sharon Wegscheider, Charles Deutsch, and Claudia Black have recorded the suffering in the present and future lives of children of alcoholics. A prevention program seeks to identify these children and to help them understand the source of their pain.

Children may not always realize how different their family life is until they attend school and come in contact with the families of their classmates. The fights, the tensions, the abrupt mood changes may be taken by children as normal (but no less painful). With children's growing awareness of the serious problems in the family and their relationship to alcohol may come a desire to protect the chemically-dependent parent from scrutiny. The desire is often encouraged by the non-alcoholic spouse, known as the co-dependent (Cermak, 1984), as well as the alcoholic. Ignoring their own tremendous anxiety, anger, and frustration, or expressing it in inappropriate, anti-social ways, children of alcoholics go about the business of repressing their real feelings and supporting the family lie. The denial exacts a terrible toll on their emotional development and self-expression, the effects of which echo and resonate throughout their lives. (Black, 1986).

The characteristics of children of alcoholics vary, which can make the task of identifying and reaching out especially difficult (Morehouse, 1979). Certainly acting-out, rebellious children who give the appearance of being neglected physically or emotionally should raise concerns about a possible drinking problem in the home. Even when the children's appearances are clean and tidy, their clothes may not be appropriate to the weather or the season.

Overachieving, highly compliant youngsters or adolescents whose performance fluctuates widely should cause concern for teachers. Unlike students who demand so much of the teachers' and guidance counselors' time because of inappropriate behavior, overachieving, compliant children, or inconsistent, distant children may not appear to come from a troubled family, or more specifically, from a family troubled by alcohol problems. Such students hide the disease through a forfeiture of self-expression which teachers may misinterpret as respect for authority in the case of overly compliant children or flightiness and poor study habits in the case of inconsistent students. Working with these children calls for the teachers to look beyond the apparent behaviors for the people inside the roles. Patience, obvious caring, and letting children gradually develop trust will lead the way to an open discussion of what is so fiercely protected but hurtful to their well-being.

A marked unwillingness to talk about the family, especially one parent, immediate and at times artful excuses for a parent's unresponsiveness, an overly dutiful attitude and perhaps a preference for adults contrast with most children's less uniform behavior in these areas. Cultural factors and such sensitive matters as the parent's legal status in the country can influence children's willingness to discuss home life. Nevertheless, children with a marked reluctance to relate home matters in school or whose parents are never available may be shielding a parent with a drug problem.

Children whose behavior and style are fixed and rigid in school (always the class clown; always respectful; always quiet) may be demonstrating more than an inordinate degree of consistency for one so young. The absence of a range and depth of roles may indicate the essential quality of that role to their survival at home. It is the predictability, the fixed constancy of attitude and behavior which may prompt further investigation. Children that lock into a certain, limited style of acting view the world in an equally limiting way. Teachers and guidance counselors should wonder why.

REFERRAL

Intervention counseling requires special training and credentials. Classroom teachers are not expected to work with seriously troubled youngsters and their families. Counseling is a fulltime task which cannot be assumed by administrators or guidance counselors with other duties. Troubled students and their families demand a focused intensity which should not be diluted by other pressures and responsibilities. Moreover, the referral of these students to community-based health and mental-health agencies and the case management work between the school and the community service provider place inordinate demands on intervention counselors' time and availability.

A residual benefit for the school in developing an intervention capacity is that the referral system, which may be fragmented and individualized, can be centralized and professionalized. Many teachers have had the experience of knowing students who need help but because of the pressures of time and limited resources, they are not helped. An active intervention component as a part of PIER provides the vehicle to assist these children.

Teachers play a central role, in fact the pivotal role in the intervention process, by identifying and referring students in need. While the identification of an at risk or substance abusing youngster receives a fair amount of attention at faculty inservice days, certain aspects bear repeating. Teachers assay students based on observable behavior. Performance and objective reports of behavior offer evidence of a burgeoning problem for a student. A referral containing accounts of behavior provides invaluable information to the case worker.

Teachers base academic decisions on observable behaviors. Radical changes in students' behavior alert teachers to look more deeply for symptoms. The following changes in behavior may signal to teachers that students are seeking help for some problem: sudden change in academic performance; a shift in peer group; a change in the quality of the interaction with other students (more confrontational or less engaged); increased lateness; unexplained absences; incomplete assignments; less productive work on Mondays and Fridays; changes in music and dressing habits. Concentrating needlessly on proving the existence of a problem may distant teachers from their chief role in this area which is merely to observe and record changed behaviors. Using the areas that teachers know best such as grades, assignments, conduct, and peer group relationships will reveal students in trouble.

Although a larger amount of time is spent on the signs and symptoms of drug use, relatively little time is sometimes spent on the use of this information to effect a referral. Some writers and inservice directors assume that teachers know how to do this, that the process is straightforward and simple with relatively few risks. This may not be true. The assessment and referral of youngsters for help can be a difficult, exacting process which may take an enormous toll on teachers when not handled correctly.

In referral work teachers assume a different role which poses its own difficulties. Referring teachers offer the first promise of help, that the pain, anger, and weariness can be dispelled if those in trouble truly seek change. In such a process, teachers go beyond the usual limits of interaction with students and get in touch with their pain. Teachers present the gift of hope, the belief in the ability of the students to change and be transformed. The hurting children may not hear the message so the offer must be extended repeatedly. At times the referring teachers may doubt the ability of the students to commit themselves to reform. However, the message once received can be the gift of life itself. To do this teachers need great patience and faith.

Referral Process

The referral process can be described in three stages which are designed not only to increase the prospect of a successful referral but to ensure that the referrers remain healthy throughout the process.

Step 1: Assessment -   The first stage is the assessment phase in which teachers focus on students' behavior to bring into sharp relief the previously unformed, underdeveloped notion that indeed something is going on with the students. The hardest part of an assessment for teachers may be finding the time to do it. The enormous demands on their time and energy conflict with the quiet, reflective time needed to review students' performance and behavior. Teachers frequently carry around a vague notion or undeveloped intuition about certain students which never gets fully realized. When students get in trouble teachers recognize the pattern which had nagged at the fringes of their minds but never quite coalesced. Assessment takes advantage of teachers' intuition as a starting point for examining the possibility of the need for a referral.

Many teachers rely on quick and dirty assessments which get passed along to a guidance counselor in the hall, at a faculty meeting or during some other chance meeting. Teachers may then exclude themselves from the helping process. Since the assessments are rarely thorough, the teachers remain with unfinished and half-formed thoughts which if followed might prove useful to the counselor and the student. Finally, because of their non-involvement with the students, the referral processes which were initiated by these teachers out of concern may be perceived by the students as a lack of concern. Students view the teachers as uncaring because of a lack of direct contact. In the process, the students lose important support and allies in their teachers.

Teachers need quiet time to review the students' behavior and their performance as a pre-requisite to help. If the teachers have a hunch that something is going on, time spent crystallizing the hunch behaviorally sets the stage for a successful referral. It also relieves the teachers of the nagging, unfulfilled sense about students. In fact a regular review of all students in which teachers recall recent inter-actions and observations as well as review all student performance proves very beneficial.

Step 2: Confrontation - Once teachers confirm through assessment that indeed the recent changes in stu-dents' behavior are causes for concern, they confront the students for the purpose of referral. The second stage, confrontation, is where many teachers experience difficulty. What may have seemed eminently clear after a brief but thorough review of the facts now appears garbled in the presence of defensive, resistant students, or even worse, defensive, resistant and angry parents. Teachers may be-come defensive too as the students or parents pull out all stops in questioning the teachers' assessments and motiva-tions. Teachers feel more and more compelled to justify their assessments as positions harden and tempers flare. Everyone leaves with a headache and a vow not to go through this again.

The term confrontation accurately describes the con-cept. It implies a directness that is integral to the referring or helping process, particularly as it relates to substance abusers and substance abusing families. Attempts to deli-cately elicit students' problems through non-directive, open-ended questioning do not produce the expected result. Substance abusers and their families have mastered the art of non-directness and avoidance. Explanations for problems abound, except the appropriate one. Whatever the problem may appear to be it is never related to the use of drugs or alcohol.

Attempts by teachers to elicit the real reason or to understand the cause of the problem may tie them in knots and make the acceptance of the referral more difficult. A confrontation is a direct interaction between the individual teacher and the student and/or the parent in which discrepancies in the student's observed behavior and performance are raised for the purpose of moving the student into a helping, ongoing counseling relationship. The confrontation seeks to offer immediate help to the student (not to generate more data), to confirm the existence and nature of a problem or to relieve tensions and troubles.

While confrontation denotes a directness between teachers and students, it does not imply an angry clashing of wills in which a winner and a loser emerge. Confronting students does not mean convincing them of how right the teachers are.

Elements in confrontation process - A confrontation contains five elements which I have labeled the 5C's of confrontation. If teachers keep these elements uppermost in their minds, the chances for successful referrals increase.

1. Clarity of purpose - The assessment of the individual student has led to this confrontation which in turn will lead to an exploration of the student's and possibly the family's need for ongoing counseling with specially trained staff. The confrontation does not provide help; it offers it. Teachers can confuse the two and in the process find themselves helping very troubled students who may divulge personal material which teachers may not be trained to handle. Some children see the concern of caring adults as the opportunity to unburden themselves. Teachers who are unclear about their role may be flattered by the children's trust and mistakenly confuse symptom relief for problem resolution.

Substance abusers seem to be able to sense the vulnerability of some teachers who need to be needed and they exploit them as a means of immobilizing one of the few forces at work that is moving them toward change. Teachers and those making referrals must be clear that the purpose of the confrontation is limited and that self-disclosure by students should serve that purpose only. Once a primary counseling relationship is established, the student-teacher relationship affords an excellent support for the counseling. Any other purpose runs the very serious danger of meeting more teachers' needs than students'.

2. Concrete and Current Feedback - Current examples of performance and behavior stand a better chance of being heard by students than examples that spring from the past. All people have a way of forgetting the past, especially the negative past. Vague or overgeneralized feedback tends to be rejected by the listener. Excuses can always be found or given for vague statements. The assessment provides concrete examples of teachers' concerns for the students. Vague and historical references provide the drug abusing students with opportunities to reject the feedback because it lacks specificity and happened in the past.

3. Concern - Teachers recognize changes in students' attendance or grades, although few teachers can use these changes to motivate students to seek help for a drug abusing problem. The difference is the level of concern which reflects a genuine expression of caring which goes beyond grades and behavior to the person. Troubled students test this commitment all the time, in the classroom as well as the confrontation. They must see teachers as advocates, as persons who somehow see through to their turmoil. If the concern isn't genuine the teachers won't be believed. Teachers who insert themselves into students' personal lives via a confrontation have made a commitment to those students beyond what is ordinary. Teachers should realize this before engaging the students and then should demonstrate it during the confrontation.

4. Contract - Sometimes referrals can't be completed in one session. A student may open up and the teacher must listen (without losing sight of the goal), or the student may resist the opportunity without dismissing it completely out of hand. Ambivalence about getting help is common among substance abusers and families who are afraid to examine their drug use no matter how bad things may have gotten. A confrontation which breaks through the wall of denial may lead to more talk with no commitment for anything else. Building trust takes time and teachers have to be prepared to give it.

In protracted referrals, teachers must be certain of what they are agreeing to and be equally sure that the children understand as well. Contracts for some time-limited sessions leading to a decision about getting help or taking some other positive step (e.g. joining a prevention activity) assure all the parties that they can continue with the task at hand without unvoiced expectations by either party undercutting or distorting the process. Contract for a specified number of sessions can take the burden off teachers to accomplish everything in a single session with students. Over the period of the contracts the students (or parents) come to grips with the immediate circumstances which have affected their current performance and hopefully see the advantage of further help. Whatever the outcome, contracts protect teachers from backing into a counseling relationship through an open-ended, undefined commitment.

5. Confidentiality - Contracts also allow for a serious discussion of the rules and limitations of confidentiality so that teachers do not find themselves in very strained circumstances concerning students' right to privacy and teachers' responsibilities to the school. What is kept confidential and in what degree (absolute confidentiality; informing the guidance or intervention counselor of their talks) should be understood by both parties if they are going to talk about personal matters over a period of time.

The 5C's of confrontation enable teachers to use their relationships with students to get the youngsters help. Regardless of the outcome a confrontation can be an emotional experience which challenges abilities and exposes fragilities. The effects of the experience are not unilateral. Talking to young people or parents about highly-charged, personal matters has an impact on the referrers who often have no place to examine and discharge their thoughts and emotions generated by the experiences. The third stage in the referral process is solely for the benefit of referrers: Personal Closure.

Step 3: Personal Closure - Although the fall-out from the confrontation affects both parties, the effects are usually acknowledged only for one side. Nevertheless, the referrers' reactions to the experience can be as personal and highly intense as the persons being referred. Previously unrealized perspectives about their childhood, or more immediate concerns about themselves, families, relationships, and occupations can be stimulated in the process of providing help, yet rarely are there opportunities to bring personal closure to the experiences. There may be an emotional hangover at times to referral work which goes largely unacknowledged in the process. The personal resolution phase completes for the referrers the process that was begun for students.

Although any number of ways to resolve the personal dimension of the referral process (talking with a close friend; thinking about the issues; working out the physical tension) exist, an excellent tool is journal writing. Teachers use the journal to write personal accounts of the experiences as they relate to themselves. Memories, feelings, thoughts (both good and bad, both old and new) are summarized and written down. The act of externalizing their reactions on paper often serves to minimize their impact and vitality. Regardless of the outcome of the referral, the personal closure phase puts some perspective and distance to the matter, thereby completing the process.

The personal closure phase works against the very dangerous assumption in referral work which equates effectiveness with completed referrals. Teachers, no more or less than other humans, cannot force people to seek help, or once sought, to benefit from the counseling. The best that can be done is to offer help out of a sense of commitment. Counselors and teachers who determine their value by the actions of those they seek to help overstate their own influence and inevitably understate their own worth. Teachers can be very effective at assessing and confronting troubled students but no one gets helped. The personal closure phase enables them to develop perspective, even to lament their limitations and the intransigence of the human condition. It is also the place to acknowledge the spirit and honesty of the effort. Personal closure ties together the loose ends, psychological or otherwise, so that referrers can move ahead without a debilitating sense of futility or anxiety from their efforts to motivate others toward health.

The three stage process of referral - assessment, confrontation, and personal closure - utilizes teachers' strengths in mobilizing troubled students or families to get help, while defining the involvement and minimizing the after-effects for teachers in the process. For teachers who may have little interest in an active role in the education, prevention, or intervention components of the PIER program, the three stage referral process offers an invaluable way to contribute to the school and to the students in greatest need.

REFERENCES

Black, C. (1979). Children of alcoholics. *Alcohol Health and Research World, Fall.* 23-27.

_____ (1986). *It Could Never Happen to Me.* St. Paul: Minnesota Addiction Commission.

Cermak, T.L. (1984). Children of alcoholics and the case for a new diagnostic category of codependency. *Alcohol and Health Research World, Summer,* 39 - 42.

Deutsch, C. (1982). *Broken Bottles, Broken Dreams.* New York: Teacher's College Press.

Morehouse, E. (1979). Working in the schools with children of alcoholic parents. *Health and Social Work, 4.* 145-162.

Schwartz, W. (1971). On the use of groups in social work practice. In W. Schwartz & S. Zalba (Eds.) *The Practice of Group Work.* New York: Columbia University Press.

_____ (1961). The social worker in the group. *New Perspective on Services to Groups: Theory, Organization and Practice.* New York: National Association of Social Workers.

Shields, S.A. (1986). Busted and branded : Group work with substance abusing adolescents in achools. *Journal of Social Work with Groups, 8,* 61-81.

Wegscheider, S. (1979). No one escapes from a chemically dependent family. In *Nurturing Networks.* Crystal, MN.

CHAPTER 8:
TEACHERS AS HEALERS

The story is told of the man of great faith who believed deeply in the power of God. A mighty storm caused the river near the town where he lived to jump its banks and threaten everyone living there. The first evacuation order led to a National Guard truck stopping by his house in order to bring him to safe ground. The man refused to be budged from his porch noting that, "God would provide for those who believe in him." A state of emergency was later declared. Shortly a boat came by and offered to transport the man to dry ground since the water was now reaching the second floor of the house. The man refused again, seeing the storm as a test of his faith in God. Finally, as the man clung to the antenna on his roof, a helicopter passed overhead in a last attempt to rescue the man. Again the man refused. Eventually he was swept away by the rising water. As the man was about to go down for the third time, he cried out, "Lord, save me if you will, for I have great faith in you!" This time the man received a direct answer to his prayer. "Save you?" God answered, "Who do you think sent you the truck, boat and helicopter?"

I am often struck by how much easier it is to believe in God than it is to believe in God in the world. The man of faith in this story was ready to test his faith, he was less ready to practice it. The distinction appeals to me when I consider the ministry of Catholic educators and teachers as healers. Believing in God, in Jesus, makes little difference to students if the believing remains private, if the "truck, boat, and helicopter" being sent out by the Lord to the people of faith are not seen for what they are. What good is faith if it doesn't make a difference?

Perhaps the greatest challenge for Catholic educators is to express their faith in their day to day experiences with students and to communicate God's love as they exercise their teaching ministry. No one will test that belief more sorely and reject its expression more quickly than substance abusing students.

The abuse of psychoactive substances by definition blocks and opposes any experience of faith. Substance abuse is a solipsistic experience which submerges people in an artificial, distorted reality. Their experience is essentially passive and isolating, no matter how active and connected these people feel on drugs. The external environment and the internal world are reshaped. The reality of life, its hard and soft edges, its infinite capacity to please and to pain, is turned off by people who use drugs. In some ways chronic substance abuse is the minimal response possible while continuing to breathe. It is safe because it is artificial. The joy and terror of living are reduced to a pitiful, vacuous existence. Substance abusers gradually cut themselves off from themselves, others, and ultimately God. The irony of substance abusers' credo of feeling good and being high is that ultimately chronic drug abuse is an expression of despair and the meaninglessness of life.

People of faith threaten the foundation of drug abusing students' reality. Substance abusers have narcotized themselves to the presence of the real world and to God's presence in the world. Teachers with faith see past the anger and the bitterness with which drug abusers defend themselves against any intrusion of real life on their chemical life. Teachers' unwillingness to accept the behavior of substance abusers confounds and often angers users. "Why won't the teacher accept what I have worked so hard to achieve? Why won't the teacher leave me alone with my chemicals? What does the teacher see that I don't?"

Teachers who know God's love and are willing to show it in their work challenge the certainty of drug using students. Drug abusing students are annoyed by teachers who will not accept their behavior nor play along with them. Troubled students spend most of their time developing scenarios and incidents which indeed reaffirm the nature of their unforgiving, uncaring world. These students especially relish when adults attempt to convince them otherwise, that if they would only change their behavior, be more responsible, recognize the wonderful gifts that God has given them, then they wouldn't be in such trouble. Lectures, attempts at conversions, subtle manipulations, angry confrontations only convince troubled students more of their reality.

Teachers who value students, who communicate this concern see through the eyes of faith. Teachers who can love unconditionally, as God has called us to do, and whose behavior, demeanor, expressions and attitudes show God's love may make a difference in the lives of drug abusing students.

Faith may be considered the flip-side response of the same coin as drug abuse. Faith answers in a personal way the questions, "What is my worth? Why am I here? What difference does my being in this world make?" Effective, really effective teachers with faith may be the only ones to show the students the flip-side of that coin.

Of course, the ultimate defense of cynics is the willful refusal to believe. The last bastion of personal resistance is "I don't believe you." Cynics, drug abusing students, fear that something else is going on here, that God's love is only a more subtle manipulation to get them to do what the teachers want. Drug use continues as a defiant assertion of their right to be hurtful, their right to despair.

Many troubled students manifest defiance and numbness rather than acknowledge their own vulnerability. Defiance is the final defense against knowing that people care for them, that teachers love them, that educators believe them worthwhile. Love cuts very deeply, deeper still for those who have long felt unloved and unable to love.

The infinite love of God is almost unbearable. Few of us want to get too close to this reality; it hurts too much to be so vulnerable to God's goodness. But teachers who know this are the very best teachers. They heal, not by dispelling or solving human problems but by showing a deeper reality to students. Substance abusing youth don't like people who can't be shaken in their love for them. It's too painful and exposing. It reflects God's unconditional invitation to all. Only the very best teachers are willing to show the power of the Spirit in their lives and to behold the beauty of the children that they teach.

CHAPTER 9:
PIER—HOW TO
IMPLEMENT IT

THE SCOPE OF THE NEED

The phenomenon of widespread, regular use of psychoactive substances has become almost normative in our society. Alcohol, marijuana, cocaine, tranquilizers, etc. have become the modern day tools to chase the blues, to celebrate, to chill out, to bounce back, even to try to maintain a certain performance level. The context of this "feel good through chemistry" approach is the broader message of "feel good above all else" that blares out to everyone through the advertisements and the electronic media which equate status and fulfillment with life style, mood and the acquisition of a seemingly inexhaustible list of things which promise happiness through spending.

Substance abuse is a thread running through the mosaic of modern experience. It affects the best efforts to address the modern problems of today's society. It affects the efforts to educate the young, making them unresponsive and causing some to drop out at the earliest opportunity. It is the single greatest cause of crime, either in acquiring the money to buy the drugs or in committing violent crimes under the influence. It cheats efforts of social justice as people without hope seek relief in a chemically-induced euphoria. It distorts our economy as billions of illegal, untaxed dollars compete for goods and services with legitimately earned dollars. It corrupts officials, hardens youth, destroys families and kills lives. It expresses the mindlessness and bankrupt morality that afflicts modern society.

The time has come to recognize the enormity of the problem. As chemically dependent individuals learn that they cannot restore themselves to wholeness unless they first address their substance abuse, I believe that society must confront the subtle, but no less dominant role that the use of psychoactive chemicals has come to play in daily living. The fits and starts method of drug prevention which runs in the same cycle as national and local political elections exemplifies the cynical treatment that the issue receives. With a wink and a nod, presidents, members of congress, governors and mayors announce yet another "War on Drugs" in the federal, state or local budget coinciding with their re-election year.

If there was ever a war on drugs, it has long been lost. Widespread substance abuse is no longer an acute, aberrational phenomenon affecting only youth, but a chronic, endemic condition which undercuts the best efforts of public and private institutions to address the major problems of society. This country has backed into de facto acceptance of the regular use of a host of dangerous chemicals because of its failure to confront the problem in any substantive, systemic way. The time has come to put away the rhetoric about wars and rallies and "Just Say No." It is time to call upon the planners and the funders to develop a comprehensive, sustained, self-financing substance abuse prevention system in every school and community in the United States.

NATIONAL LEVEL

Individual Catholic leaders have been among the most vocal in calling attention to the alarming levels of drug use and the need for a more sustained, organized response. Yet the national Catholic organizations have lagged behind the leadership of individual men and women in the church. The collective leadership of the Catholic Church in America needs to become a recognizable, organized force in preventing drug and alcohol abuse in society.

In recent years how much attention has the United States Catholic Conference given to this issue? What departments in this conference are charged with assisting the bishops and national Catholic leadership to address this problem? What effect would a bishops' pastoral on this topic have on the Catholic population and general population? What highly visible actions have other national Catholic welfare and educational agencies taken in this area?

What actions have religious communities of men and women taken to assist those in their communities and those they serve? What guidance have national lay organizations provided?

The creation of a national Catholic office on substance abuse would acknowledge that so important a matter as the prevention of drug use will not be left to chance or the vagaries of politics. Moreover, such an office can become the forum to examine the widespread debilitating effects of psychoactive drugs on the lives and spirits of the American people. Substance abuse strikes at the heart of basic Christian-Judaic values about the dignity of the individual and the intrinsic worth of life itself. In forging a leadership role for themselves and all peoples of faith, the American Catholic Church can speak not only to what is needed to confront the drug epidemic in America, but also to what is missing in American life that has placed children in such grave peril.

DIOCESAN LEVEL

The diocese can bring enormous energy to the issue of systematizing substance abuse prevention services in a particular state or region. It can coalesce the forces of government, education, criminal justice industry and citizen groups in a willing partnership for change.

Before individual dioceses take leadership with other groups in combatting the problems associated with drug abuse, the officials of each diocese need to evaluate their own situation in terms of preparedness to actively combat this scourge.

How informed are those who minister in the diocese of the bio/psycho/social effects of drugs? Does the diocese have an active and effective training program for those beginning the ministry and ongoing updating for those who have been ministering for several years? Are these programs offered to all who minister in the diocese? In such training programs what efforts are made to go beyond the mere dispensing of information to arrive at a sensitive understanding of the person? Do ministers view this issue as an integral part of Christian formation?

Addressing the issue of chemical dependence can be somewhat uncomfortable for some ministers. Some widely circulated research has indicated that larger numbers of clergy and others in the helping profession become addicted to alcohol. Many of these people may also have lived the trauma of an alcoholic family and may still carry the emotional burden of that experience, often unrecognized, in their daily lives. Over the last several years more and more dioceses and religious orders of men and women have taken noble, charitable steps to assist those of their members who have an addiction problem. With the increase in lay ministers, a need may exist to broaden diocesan programs. The openness with which these institutions address this concern would break through the isolation that individuals and families experience. This would be a first step to restoring them to full health, bodily and spiritually.

Since education is a major component in the prevention of drug abuse, the diocesan offices of education need to take positive steps to address the dimensions of the problem in its system, to assist schools in the development of programs and to monitor their progress.

An advisory committee to the chief educational officials of the diocese could be established. This body would suggest diocesan guidelines on substance abuse issues in the schools and parish religious education programs, review the curriculum and its placement in school and parish religious education programs, formulate a comprehensive inservice program for teachers and catechists, propose major events such as rallies, health fairs, or conferences to bring attention to the need, monitor all aspects of substance abuse as it relates to young Catholics in the parishes.

On a regular basis the diocesan office needs to conduct a study of drug usage patterns among the youth. This could be done every four years for all students in school and parish religious education programs in grades 5 to 12. While the anonymity of each student must be preserved, this periodic survey can provide invaluable data for developing a systemwide perspective on drug usage and a gauge of future needs.

This advisory committee may suggest the need of a full-time person to serve as a field representative to the various programs of the diocese, to seek additional funding for projects, and to keep the advisory committee knowledgeable of the problem.

The advisory committee should also work to secure funds to carry on its various programs. Part of this search includes an active investigation of funding sources on the local, state and federal levels. A second task would be seeking to secure a formula based funding approach. The prevention services must be developed on a per capita formula driven basis which assigns dollars automatically to all schools because of the society's overriding interest in preventing drug use among its young people. Such funding needs to be available to all children because it seeks to promote good health not religion.

ROLE OF THE PRINCIPAL

Experience has shown that the leadership of the principal makes the prevention program work in a school. Dedicated teachers make a difference in the lives of their students, the home school association involves parents, but the principal alone can assemble the tripod of home-school-community cooperation.

The resistance from various elements in the school can make the prevention program a real chore. Faculty members may view working with students affectively as somehow soft or coddling; janitors may not want to keep the building open for the Al-a-non and Al-a-Teen meetings after school; parents may want to hear only about the school's program for the "gifted"; students may view this effort as a new way to test the disciplinary procedures. Through all of this, the principal continues to breathe life into the program, hold hands when necessary, and demand accountability of all. The principal communicates the need for the program to all. The principal starts the process of introducing a PIER-type program into the school.

Although the principal is the fulcrum for bringing the prevention services into a school, the principal should not be directly involved in them, especially in those areas where students discuss personal matters. The authority of the administrator can be too easily compromised when information is received through channels which prevent the principal from acting upon it.

ROLE OF THE STUDENTS

The second most important group in the development of a program is the students. Students need to provide input into the establishment of the program and seek to create a unanimity of purpose. Not always do the members of the student council or other recognized student leaders provide the leadership and this unanimity. Often the troubled students and those they associate with are the first to see some benefits in the activities of such a program.

Beginning in pre-adolescence, youngsters become very conscious of adult attempts at limiting freedom and are skeptical of even the most benign efforts. The only way to ensure that all the work and effort do not fail because of student unresponsiveness is to involve students from the beginning in fashioning a response. Parents need to be included as well since they are often asked to do more as a result of the prevention effort.

ROLE OF THE FACULTY

For a whole host of reasons some individual faculty members may resent and resist prevention programming in a school. Too much time out of class, not enough time for the basics, the program is unnecessary, ineffective, disruptive, too protective, the list can go on and on. While some complaints are valid, others mask fears and prejudices.

Faculty members need also to feel part of the process, that their insights have been sought and incorporated into the program. Faculty members play a double role in the program. First, they support the program with their words, actions and attitudes. Having been involved in the formulation of the program, they both see its value and appreciate the need for their complete support of the program. Second, most often the teachers will be the first people that discover trouble students. Their keen observations and sensitivities to growing adolescents enable prevention and remediation efforts to begin as soon as they are manifested. Because of the sensitive role that they play they know both the importance of being well informed in the area and of responding with care to students. Without the support of the faculty the program will go nowhere.

NEED FOR SPECIAL PERSON

In most schools no person has the special skills and appropriate set of other responsibilities to do the work of drug prevention. A guidance counselor, school psychologist, health educator, or school social worker comes closest by discipline and training. While such persons may exist in a school, they usually have extensive duties which limit their availability. A separate person to develop and run the prevention program, with costs paid by several schools involved in this program, is perhaps the best way to develop a program quickly. This person needs to understand the role of education and the school in children's lives, as well as the unique role of Catholic education. A program will fail if the employed person remains unfamiliar with the school setting and mission. The person needs to imbibe the school philosophy, teaching methods, testing program, policy on discipline, confidentiality and collegiality.

CHAPTER 10: THE FIVE KNOWS OF DRUG ABUSE FOR PARENTS

More than anyone else involved in Catholic education, parents need to be heard on the dangers facing their children. Parents may even need to educate the school leadership to the urgency of their need. The commitment to a planned, ongoing program manifests itself when parents speak out about the nearly impossible challenge they confront in trying to raise drug-free children in this society. While parents need help, improved parenting skills alone are not enough. A home-school-community collaboration provides the discipline, limits the availability of drugs and offers the alternatives to the "get high through chemical" approach to life.

Parents who believe that proper upbringing alone will prevent their children's involvement are not fully aware of the realities of growing up in America. The risk-taking and pseudo-adult behavior of today's teenagers cannot be compared to the dangers of the past. Parents have a right to insist on their children receiving the proper services to complement their proper upbringing at home. The tripod of home-school-community will not be established without the direct and insistent leadership of parents struggling to raise drug-free children.

The parental indifference and apathy explanation for widespread teenage drug use always seemed a bit too neat to me. Words like *pressure, demands,* and *overwhelmed* come closer to the truth about parental attitudes toward youthful drug abuse. I have spoken to frightened and frustrated parents. They have so much to protect a child from, so much to teach. Taking on one more task seems almost impossible. Parents may consequently ignore or misinterpret the children's behavior. Parents deny as children deny the impact of the substance abuse on their lives.

No magical formulas or instant solutions to helping children through the difficult decisions regarding drug use exist. Like people in recovery, parents take one day at a time with much love and prayers for patience and wisdom. The ingredients that foster any successful, healthy relationship apply to the parent-child relationship. These include love, trust, flexibility, limit setting and open communications.

Parents and children work together to maintain open communications. Children may become confused about their changing relationship with parents. On the other hand, children demonstrate even less consistency to the parents who view their children as children today but view them as adults tomorrow. Nevertheless the relationship survives despite all the twists and turns when it is built on trust and love and these are continually affirmed.

What are some effective strategies that can help children confront the issue of substance abuse? The "Five Knows of Drug Abuse for Parents" may be of some help.

KNOW THE FACTS

Do parents know the bio/psycho/social effects of drug use? Children can seize upon their parents' discomfort as proof positive that they know better. In fact many youngsters today, particularly the young drug consumers, are equally ignorant of a drug's risks and dangers. Concepts like tolerance (the need to take larger and larger amounts of a drug to get its original effect), synergy (the interaction of two drugs to produce an effect greater than the sum of the effects of each taken alone) and rebound (the body's corrective response in the opposite direction of the drug's effects before returning to normal functioning) can help parents engage their children in a meaningful discussion of the potential risks, based on the facts about the drug and the processes which govern the body's reaction to it. Knowing the facts provides a sound basis for an intelligent discussion between parents and children.

In separated and divorced families, both parents need to learn the facts about substance abuse and apply the same standards in talking to their children. This dual responsibility leads to a united approach and avoids the children receiving contradictory messages. Such an approach prevents children from using one parent against another.

KNOW THE CHILDREN

Many parents joke that they knew their children until about the age of thirteen and then were reintroduced to them about the age of twenty. In the intervening years, parents weren't sure who the young people occasionally visiting the home were.

Over 50 years ago, Kurt Lewin, the modern father of field learning theory, spoke about how little adolescents understood themselves, and how even the most basic interpersonal structures that a person relies on for a sense of continuity and consistency (body, voice, familiar circumstances) betray adolescents. Parents don't know their adolescent children because the youngsters don't know themselves either. Youth do develop a sense of maturity and consistency over time and after failed attempts with their new behavior. Meanwhile parents need patience, flexibility and a sense of humor at each new incarnation of their teenage children.

Despite the endless changes, the moodiness and the abrupt shifts in attitudes and style, parents usually can still relate to the basic nature of their children which doesn't change in the growing process. Some parents whose children developed drug problems sensed a basic shift in their children's behaviors and personalities before the drug problem surfaced. Parents knew something was wrong with their children because they were no longer acting like themselves. Drug abuse changes people more dramatically than the changes of adolescents. Changes that cannot easily be explained may indicate a far deeper problem.

The following are some questions that parents may ask themselves about their children. Has a sudden change in their children's peer group occurred? Are the youngsters in the present peer group very different from the previous friends and group? Has a dramatic change in school performance occurred or a continued deterioration in grades over time happened? Have the number of absences from school or other settings increased? Have generally cooperative children become difficult and sullen? Have basic changes in behavior appeared, e.g. talkative children becoming silent and withdrawn, athletic and artistic children losing interest in these activities? What physical changes are evident, e.g., weight loss, loss of appetite, inability to sleep? Are things missing from the house?

While many of the changes implied in these questions do not exclusively suggest a drug problem, when the changes appear in fixed patterns and are consistently negative, then a possibility exists that some chemical problem may be present. Confronting such children and expecting honest answers are first steps in the process of getting help for the children.

Parents should have clear expectations of their children's behavior. Teens need limits. They need someone to set clear limits. The limits reflect a hierarchy of parental values which allow the youngsters the autonomy to modify and adapt the less vital matters to suit their need while at the same time recognizing those areas which cannot be transgressed. The clearer parents are on matters of importance and matters that have room for negotiation, the better teenagers will respond. Involving the children where possible in establishing ground rules and enforcing the rules consistently help both parents and children to respect each other.

KNOW CHILDREN'S FRIENDS AND PARENTS

Parents who know their children's friends have another way of knowing their children. The single best predictor of a youngster's involvement with a drug is the use or non-use of that drug by their peer group. Therefore, a very good way of knowing what children do or think is to know their peer group firsthand.

I remember speaking to a group of parents one evening about the importance of this approach in understanding their children when a hand shot up from the audience to ask advice on how to go about meeting her child's friends. This parent had an open door policy for her son and his friends and continually urged him to bring his group over to hang around or to have a party. The child never wanted to take his mother up on this offer. Why? The parent was the only one of her son's high school peer group who would not allow the adolescents to drink in her home and who would stay at home when they came over.

The single most difficult point for parents of teenagers to accept is that other people have more influence over their children's behavior than they do. While they recognize the power of the children's peer group in forming attitudes, they sometimes fail to see that their children experience multiple influences that affect what they do. Rock stars, neighborhood heroes, older adolescents and even other parents may have more influence with children than their own parents. What is particularly jarring is that unless parents of children in the same circle of friends can come to some consensus on rules governing such issues as drinking and supervised parties, an individual parent's stance can be undercut or circumvented. The mother in my audience who had clear, established rules against drinking never had a chance to exercise them because other parents did not support them. Parents of teens must know the parents of their children's friends, and they must agree on some basic rules governing house gatherings, if they are to have any success in setting limits for their children.]

KNOW ONE'S OWN VALUES

Often parents want to exclude their own behaviors and attitudes from scrutiny when setting clear expectations for their children. "Do as I say, not as I do" is never effective with children. In the area of substance abuse, this attitude is dangerous. If parents abuse alcohol, their words of caution on the dangers of substance abuse will ring hollow. The role that drugs, all drugs - legal and illegal - play in parents' lives, and how parents deal with the complexities and demands of daily living speak more loudly than any words.

As parents prepare to help their children through a very difficult period in which the allure of drug and alcohol use may appear quite compelling, they need take an honest look at their own values and behaviors. If parental behaviors give the wrong message, steps need to be taken to correct the message. Parents are the first and best teachers in this regard. They model appropriate behaviors for their children.

KNOW HOW TO GET HELP

Parents should not struggle on their own with a substance abuse problem in the family. Substance abuse problems can be resolved when they are shared. Beliefs that the problem is only temporary, the situation will turn around, or maybe the evidence does not indicate a substance abuse problem only delay the remedy. Parents need not be experts to determine what is and what is not a problem. If a spouse, child or someone parents care about has a problem, the realization that they are not alone and that others are available to assist provides powerful comfort.

Al-a-Non groups provide support for the families of alcoholics and Al-a-Teen groups provide support for the teenagers with drinking problems. The telephone numbers of such organizations can be found in the local telephone directory.

A growing number of groups exist for the adult children of alcoholics, as well as recovery groups for just about every type of drug abused by humans. State agencies dealing with alcohol and drug problems exist to provide help. These too list themselves in telephone directories.

Finally, the school can direct the counseling and substance abuse agencies in other communities to assist people in sorting out the issues related to a potential or actual drug problem. A real danger exists when people hesitate or minimize what is going on. Seeking help for oneself or another may be the most significant action of a person's lifetime.

ABOUT THE AUTHOR

Frank McCorry began ministering in Catholic education in 1969 as a teacher. In 1976 he was appointed the Director of the Archdiocese of New York Drug Abuse Prevention Program (ADAPP). This program was recognized by the state of New York in 1979 with a Certificate of Excellence. This was the first such substance abuse program to be so recognized by the state.

Frank McCorry received his doctorate from St. John's University in counseling and human services in 1982. Currently he is the Director of the AIDS Resource Unit for the New York State Division of Substance Abuse Services. He continues to lecture and consult on substance abuse prevention and AIDS issues and has been featured at the NCEA Convention.

Dr. McCorry lives in Westchester County, New York, with his wife and four children.

INDEX